Maynooth Research Guides for Irish Local History

IN THIS SERIES

1   Raymond Refaussé, *Church of Ireland Records*
2   Terry Dooley, *Sources for the History of Landed estates in Ireland*
3   Patrick J. Corish and David Sheehy, *Records of the Catholic Church in Ireland*
4   Jacinta Prunty, *Maps and Mapmaking in Local History*

Maynooth Studies in Irish Local History

IN THIS SERIES

1   Paul Connell, *Parson, Priest and Master: National Education in Co. Meath 1824–41*

2   Denis A. Cronin, *A Galway Gentleman in the Age of Improvement: Robert French of Monivea, 1716–79*

3   Brian Ó Dálaigh, *Ennis in the 18th Century: Portrait of an Urban Community*

4   Séamas Ó Maitiú, *The Humours of Donnybrook: Dublin's Famous Fair and its Suppression*

5   David Broderick, *An Early Toll-Road: The Dublin–Dunleer Turnpike, 1731–1855*

6   John Crawford, *St Catherine's Parish, Dublin 1840–1900: Portrait of a Church of Ireland Community*

7   William Gacquin, *Roscommon Before the Famine: The Parishes of Kiltoom and Cam, 1749–1845*

8   Francis Kelly, ... *Granard, Co. Longford, 1933–68*

9   Charles V. Smit...................... *all Medieval Irish Town*

10   Desmond J. C...................... *Society in Nineteenth-Century Celbri...*

11   Proinnsíos Ó Duigneáin, *The Priest and the Protestant Woman*

12   Thomas King, *Carlow: the manor and town, 1674–1721*

13   Joseph Byrne, *War and Peace: The Survival of the Talbots of Malahide 1641–1671*

14   Bob Cullen, *Thomas L. Synnott: The Career of a Dublin Catholic 1830–70*

15   Helen Sheil, *Falling into Wretchedness: Ferbane in the late 1830s*

Maynooth Studies in Irish Local History (cont.)

16   Jim Gilligan, *Graziers and Grasslands: Portrait of a Rural Meath Community 1854–1914*

17   Miriam Lambe, *A Tipperary Estate: Castle Otway, Templederry 1750–1853*

18   Liam Clare, *Victorian Bray: A Town Adapts to Changing Times*

19   Ned McHugh, *Drogheda before the Famine: Urban Poverty in the Shadow of Privilege 1826–45*

20   Toby Barnard, *The Abduction of a Limerick Heiress: Social and political relations in mid eighteenth-century Ireland*

21   Seamus O'Brien, *Famine and Community in Mullingar Poor Law Union, 1845–1849: Mud Huts and Fat Bullocks*

22   Séamus Fitzgerald, *Mackerel and the Making of Baltimore, Co. Cork, 1879–1913*

23   Íde Ní Liatháin, *The Life and Career of P.A. McHugh, 1859–1909: A Footsoldier of the Party*

24   Miriam Moffitt, *The Church of Ireland Community of Killala and Achonry 1870–1940*

25   Ann Murtagh, *Portrait of a Westmeath Tenant Community, 1879–85: The Barbavilla Murder*

26   Jim Lenehan, *Politics and Society in Athlone, 1830–1885: A Rotten Borough*

27   Anne Coleman, *Riotous Roscommon: Social Unrest in the 1840s*

28   Maighréad Ní Mhurchadha, *The Customs and Excise service in Fingal, 1684–1765: Sober, Active and Bred to the Sea*

29   Chris Lawlor, *Canon Frederick Donovan's Dunlavin 1884–1896: A west Wicklow village in the late nineteenth century*

30   Eithne Massey, *Prior Roger Outlaw of Kilmainham*

31   Terence A.M. Dooley, *The Plight of the Monaghan Protestants, 1912–26*

32   Patricia Friel, *Frederick Trench, 1746–1836 and Heywood, Queen's County the creation of a romantic landscape*

33   Tom Hunt, *Portlaw, county Waterford 1825–76, Portrait of an industrial village and its cotton industry.*

34   Brian Gurrin, *A century of struggle in Delgany and Kilcole: An exploration of the social implications of population change in north-east Wicklow, 1666–1779*

CHURCH OF IRELAND RECORDS

Maynooth Research Guides for Irish Local History

GENERAL EDITOR   Mary Ann Lyons

This pamphlet is one of three in the newly instituted Maynooth Guides for Local History series. Written by specialists in the relevant fields, these volumes are designed to provide historians, and specifically those interested in local history, with practical advice regarding the consultation of specific collections of historical material, thereby enabling them to conduct independent research in a competent and thorough manner. In each volume, a brief history of the relevant institutions is provided and the principal primary sources are identified and critically evaluated, with specific reference to their usefulness to the local historian. Readers receive step by step guidance as to how to conduct their research and are alerted to some of the problems which they might encounter in working with particular collections. Possible avenues for research are suggested and relevant secondary works are also recommended.

I wish to acknowledge the support and interest in this series shown by Dr John Logan, University of Limerick and the valuable input of Dr Raymond Gillespie, N.U.I. Maynooth and Dr Jimmy Kelly, St Patrick's College, Drumcondra.

Maynooth Research Guides for Irish Local History: Number 1

Church of Ireland Records

Raymond Refaussé

IRISH ACADEMIC PRESS
DUBLIN • PORTLAND, OR

First published in 2000 by
IRISH ACADEMIC PRESS
44, Northumberland Road, Dublin 4, Ireland
and in the United States of America by
IRISH ACADEMIC PRESS
c/o ISBS, 5804 NE Hassalo Street, Portland, OR 97213–3644.

website: www.iap.ie

British Library Cataloguing in Publication Data

Refaussé, Raymond
　　Church of Ireland records. – (Maynooth guides to local history research)
　　1. Church of Ireland.　　2. Church records and registers – Ireland.
　　I. Title
　　929.3 415

　　ISBN 0–7165–2701–4

Library of Congress Cataloging-in-Publication Data
Refaussé, Raymond, 1950–
　　Church of Ireland records / Raymond Refaussé.
　　　　p.　　cm. — (Maynooth guides for local history research)
　　Includes bibliographical references (p.) and index.
　　ISBN 0–7165–2701–4 (paperback)
　　1. Church of Ireland—Archives. 2. Church of Ireland—History—Archival
resources—Directories. 3. Church archives—Ireland—Administration. 4. Church
archives—Ireland—Directories. 5. Ireland—Church history—Archival
resources—Directories.　I. Title.　II. Series.

CD1118.5.A1 R34 2000
027.6'7 '09415—dc21　　　　　　　　　　　　　　　　　　　00–025015

Typeset in 10 pt on 12 pt Bembo by
Carrigboy Typesetting Services, County Cork
Printed by ColourBooks Ltd, Dublin

Contents

List of illustrations   vii

Acknowledgements   ix

Introduction   1

1   The administration, archives and manuscripts of the
        Church of Ireland   3
      I.   The Church in Ireland: from earliest times to the
            Reformation   3
      II.   The Church of Ireland 'As by Law Established':
            from the Reformation to 1871   11
      III. The Church of Ireland as a voluntary Christian
            community: from 1871 to the present   27

2   Access to the archives and manuscripts of the Church of Ireland   33
      I.   Intellectual access: histories, catalogues and editions   33
      II.   Physical access: visiting the libraries and archives   42

3   The interpretation of Church of Ireland archives and
        manuscripts   52

Conclusion   58

Notes   59

List of Illustrations

1   Map of the provinces and dioceses of the Church of Ireland   2

2   The constitutions of the diocese of Ossory, 6 October 1317, from the Red Book of Ossory, a fourteenth-century diocesan register written in Latin (R.C.B. Library D11/1/2, f.6)   9

3   The opening page of the register of the parish of St John the Evangelist, Dublin, 1619: the oldest extant parish register in Ireland (R.C.B. Library P328/1/1)   13

4   Minutes of a meeting of the vestry of the parish of St Nicholas, Cork, 22 January 1777 (R.C.B. Library P498/5/1)   19

5   Extract from the proctors' accounts of Christ Church cathedral, Dublin, showing examples of ordinary and extraordinary disbursements, 1675–5 (R.C.B. Library C6/1/15/1)   23

Acknowledgements

This guide has been written from the background of almost twenty years as the archivist of the Church of Ireland and I am enormously grateful to many clergy and laity, members of staff in Church of Ireland House, Dublin, and researchers in the Representative Church Body Library from whom I have learned much of what follows. I am indebted to my colleagues in the R.C.B Library, Susan Hood, Heather Smith and Mary Furlong, for providing much needed space from time to time, and to the Representative Church Body for permission to reproduce plates 2, 4 and 5. Plate 3 is reproduced by permission of the Director of the National Archives.

I am grateful to Raymond Gillespie who suggested this project to me and especially to the series editor, Mary Ann Lyons, whose conscientious reading of the text has saved me from many errors and has imposed a much needed uniformity of style.

My principal debt, however, is to the members of the classes of the M.A. in Local History course in N.U.I. Maynooth who have, in turn, been bored by topics which I thought to be fascinating, enthralled by things which I believed to be of no account, and who have continually asked me questions to which I did not know the answers. To them this guide is cheerfully dedicated.

RAYMOND REFAUSSÉ

Introduction

The Church is the only institution in Ireland which has survived from the earliest times to the present day predating central government, municipal corporations and the handful of educational and fraternal bodies which have been extant since the middle ages. Its longevity combined with its sustained presence in almost every corner of the country suggests that it is, or has been, the most profound influence in the formation of Irish society. Since the sixteenth century the Church in Ireland has been divided and of those parts of the Church which withdrew their allegiance from Rome the most historically significant is the Church of Ireland.

The Church of Ireland is an anglican or episcopalian church. It is a reformed catholic Church: reformed, in that it is opposed to any teaching and practice which appears to be contrary to scripture and to the teaching of the primitive Church; and catholic, in that it is in possession of a continuous tradition of faith and practice based on the scriptures and early tradition, and enshrined in the catholic creeds, the sacraments and the three fold ministry of deacons, priests and bishops. It is, legally at least, the lineal descendant of the Celtic Church, for following the Reformation it was established as the official church of the state, a situation which continued until the late nineteenth century when disestablishment reduced its status to that of a voluntary Christian community. These three phases of development – the pre-Reformation Church, the Established Church, and the disestablished Church – provide convenient divisions under which to examine the administration of the Church of Ireland and the records which that administration produced.

However, the archives (the papers which have been accumulated in the process of the official administration of the Church) and manuscripts (the records of individuals and organizations which, although Church of Ireland in orientation, are not part of the Church's official archives but complementary to them) of the Church of Ireland are not all held in one repository. Neither are they all under the control of the Church. Consequently it is not possible to describe and analyse Church of Ireland records as one distinct collection. What follows, therefore, is an overview of the Church's administration and the archives and manuscripts which it produced; a guide to the various published catalogues and printed editions; and an introduction to the principal repositories in which Church of Ireland records are to be found with an indication of the types of material contained in these institutions.

1. Map of the provinces and dioceses of the Church of Ireland

The administration, archives and manuscripts of the Church of Ireland

I. THE CHURCH IN IRELAND: FROM EARLIEST TIMES TO THE REFORMATION

The elements of what most people would consider to be the essentials of Church administration – bishops, dioceses and parishes – are the product of the early Christian Church.[1] The term bishop is an Anglo-Saxon corruption of the Greek word *episcopus* which means overseer. In the early Church the terms bishops and priests seem to have been interchangeable but by the beginning of the second century the threefold ministry of bishops, priests and deacons was becoming defined, and by the middle of the century all the leading centres of Christianity would appear to have had bishops, the particular functions of whom were to ordain to holy orders and to confirm the baptised. The unit of administration which a bishop governed was the diocese and in the early Church, when Christianity was an urban religion, dioceses were small in extent, covering only the principal towns and cities. However, as the Church expanded into rural areas the limits of the dioceses were extended until all the civilized world was, notionally at least, within the jurisdiction of a diocesan bishop. In the western Church the term *parochia*, which is, of course, the origin of the word parish, was used in some places to describe the bishop's area of jurisdiction but from the later fourth century it came to be applied to the subdivisions of the diocese which the bishop put in the charge of resident priests. By the seventh century the parochial system had spread as far as England.[2] In Ireland, however, ecclesiastical jurisdictions were arranged differently. The Celtic Church was not diocesan but monastic and monasteries rather than parish churches were the centres of Christian life. Bishops were needed to ordain and confirm and so they remained a part of the Irish ecclesiastical polity but they generally lived in the monasteries and were subject to the rule of the abbot.

The written legacy of the Celtic Church lies not so much in what we would understand as archives but in monastic annals such as the Annals of Inisfallen and the Annals of Tigernach which can provide valuable data on chronology, and hagiographical lives of the saints like St Fin Barre of Cork and the various St Patricks, which can often give an interesting sense of a

3

locality. Also valuable are liturgical and related manuscripts beginning, probably, with the Cathach, an austere sixth-century psalter, and reaching its apogee in the splendidly illuminated ninth-century gospel book, the Book of Kells. Insofar as these manuscripts have survived they are to be found not in the custody of the Church of Ireland but in the great national and university collections in Ireland, Great Britain and continental Europe, for following the dissolution of the monasteries in the sixteenth century the contents of the their libraries were widely dispersed. The Church of Ireland, as the legal lineal successor of the Church in Ireland, might have been expected to have inherited many of these treasures but, for the most part, this was not the case. The reformed Church of Ireland was puritan in outlook and cared little for such things, and even those items, which by default, remained in the Church's custody or subsequently came into its possession were largely alienated in later centuries. For example, Henry Jones, bishop of Meath, removed the Book of Kells from Kells in 1653 and donated it to Trinity College, Dublin, while in 1854 Lord John George Beresford, archbishop of Armagh, gave the Book of Armagh to the college.[3]

The idyllic world of the Celtic Church was rudely disturbed by the Viking invasions from the late eighth century but ironically it was these seemingly iconoclastic incursions which provided the motivation for a reform of the Irish Church in the twelfth century that would bring its administration more into line with the western European model. The subsequent settlement of the Danes in Ireland in the eleventh century and their conversion to Christianity, most probably by missionaries from Scandavanian Britain, led to the appointment of bishops in Dublin, Waterford and Limerick who were subject to the authority of Canterbury rather than Armagh. In particular the consecration, in 1106, of Gilbert of Limerick, a close friend of the archbishop of Canterbury, who was later appointed papal legate, brought the Church into contact with the reform movement in continental Europe which had begun in the monastery of Cluny in France. The first substantial achievement of the reformers was in 1110 when the Synod of Rathbreasil, which was presided over by Bishop Gilbert, divided Ireland into twenty-four dioceses, in addition to the primatial see of Armagh, although the Danish diocese of Dublin was ignored. In 1148 the Synod of Inishpatrick authorized Malachy, archbishop of Armagh, to travel to Rome to receive the palium, a vestment which showed that he held his authority from the pope but he died before reaching Rome. However, in 1152 the pope sent a legate to Ireland to confer pallia on four archbishops – Armagh, Cashel, Tuam and, significantly, Dublin – so completing and regularizing the diocesan administration in Ireland.

One of the consequences of this reform of the diocesan system was a growth in the importance of cathedrals in the life of the Church.[4] The cathedral was the centre of the bishop's administration of his diocese and was the church which contained his throne (*cathedra* in Latin) or official seat. It was usually, although not necessarily, the grandest and most splendid church in the diocese and was initially in the vicinity of the bishop's residence where it was served by the bishop and his household. However, as the bishop's pastoral and administrative duties grew and as worship in the cathedral became more elaborate, responsibility for the administration of the cathedral was gradually delegated to a separate body of clergy. The result was the development of a distinct ecclesiastical corporation, or chapter, with its own rights and privileges. This was usually a secular corporation, headed by a dean, but could be a monastic body governed by a prior. In Ireland the development of the cathedral system was essentially a consequence of the Norman invasion. The Celtic Church had not accorded a pre-eminent position to bishops in its polity and so the churches which held their *cathedra* had not enjoyed a particularly high status. However, during the twelfth and thirteenth centuries existing cathedrals were rebuilt and new edifices erected according to English and continental styles of church architecture. Christ Church cathedral, Dublin was rebuilt around 1173, probably by masons from the west of England, and similar architectural influences are apparent in the cathedrals of Cashel, Kilkenny and St Patrick's, Dublin, which, together with Kildare, Down, Killaloe, Waterford and Ardfert, were built in the thirteenth century.

Just as England provided the architectural models for Irish cathedrals so too it provided the administrative model. The clergy who staffed the secular cathedrals were called canons: the word canon originally meant rule and the cathedral canons at first lived a sort of communual life even though they were not monks. During the middle ages the common life was abandoned and the endowments were divided into separate portions to support each member of the chapter. The endowments, which came from the rents, fees and tithes of parishes, were called prebends (from the Latin *praebere* – to supply) because they furnished a living for their holders. The canons came to be called prebendaries and were named after the parish which supported them: for example the prebendary of Mullabrack in St Patrick's cathedral, Armagh, or the prebendary of Aghour in St Canice's cathedral, Kilkenny.

The chief officer of the cathedral was the dean who presided over meetings of the chapter. He was, in theory, elected by the chapter but by the middle ages such appointments were usually made on the nomination of the crown. Three other officers, together with the dean, formed the *quatuor personae*, the four cornerstones of the spiritual and temporal life of the cathedral. The precentor was in charge of the services, the music and liturgy, and the choir while the chancellor kept the cathedral seal, was responsible for education in the cathedral schools, and was usually the librarian and archivist. The treasurer was not, as might be supposed from the title, a financial officer but the guardian of the cathedral treasures – plate, vestments and relics. Each of these officers had a deputy, who probably did most of the work: the sub-dean, succentor, vice-chancellor and sacrist. The principal function of the cathedral clergy was the *opus Dei*, the daily round of prayer and praise, with the celebration of the mass, several times each day as the central act of worship. As these celebrations became more elaborate they could not be maintained by the residentiary canons and their places were taken by vicars choral, that is deputies (the original meaning of the term vicar) who were skilled in singing. In most cathedrals the vicars choral developed as a separate ecclesiastical corporation from the dean and chapter and were supported by their own endowments.

All the Irish medieval cathedrals, except two, were secular and conformed, subject to local peculiarities, to the administrative model which has been outlined above. Christ Church, Dublin, and Down, however, were monastic cathedrals (Augustinian in the case of the former while Down was a Benedictine foundation) and their administration differed somewhat from their secular counterparts. Monastic cathedrals were a uniquely English phenomenon (secular arrangements were the norm in continental Europe) which had developed under the influence of St Dunstan in the tenth century. A monastic cathedral was headed by a prior. Technically an abbot was the head of a monastery but in a monastic cathedral the position of abbot was held by the bishop who was not usually a monk and so the prior, normally the second in command, was in charge. The prior was aided by a number of assistants called obedientiaries, the number of whom varied according to the size of the house. The more important of these were the sub-prior; the sacrist, who had custody of the relics, vestments and service books; the precentor, who was responsible for the music; the receiver, who gathered in the revenues from the monastic estates; the cellarer, who provided food and drink; and the almoner, who distributed relief and looked after the school for poor boys. These monastic communities were supported by the food and drink and financial returns from estates which were settled on them by monarchs, nobles and wealthy citizens who were anxious to secure for themselves and their families the prayers of the community for the repose of their souls.

Parishes in Ireland, like the cathedrals, were essentially Norman innovations. In western Europe the basis of the parochial system was the payment of tithes which were due from specific lands for the support of particular churches but tithes were not paid in Ireland before the late twelfth century. The creation of parishes proceeded in Ireland in the late twelfth and early thirteenth centuries based on Norman manors and, in the areas outside Norman settlement, on monastic lands or lands of ancient families. By the early fourteenth century the whole country, with the exception of Counties Leitrim and Longford (the diocese of Ardagh), had a network of parishes, grouped into rural deaneries which seem to have been based on old Irish territories.[5]

The archives of the medieval church in Ireland – the records of parishes, cathedrals, dioceses and their bishops – have survived only in a fragmentary manner. The unsettled state of medieval Ireland, the dislocating effects of the dissolution of the monasteries and the Reformation, and the periodic unrest to which early modern Ireland was subject were not conditions that were conducive to the accretion of archival collections.

Only two collections of medieval parish records have survived, these being from the Dublin churches of St Werburgh and St John. The St Werburgh's material consists of churchwardens' accounts from 1481 to 1520, half a dozen draft leases from the sixteenth century and a parchment folio from a thirteenth-century psalter which, it has been suggested, was used in the church: all of these items are in the Representative Church Body Library.[6] The St John's material is a collection of 203 parish deeds covering the period 1231 to 1704 which are in the Library of Trinity College, Dublin[7] and three liturgical manuscripts – two fourteenth-century processionals, one in the Bodleian Library in Oxford and the other in Marsh's Library in Dublin, and a fifteenth-century antiphonary (a book of verses sing by a choir) which is in Trinity.[8] However, the St John's liturgical manuscripts may originally have been acquired for use in Christ Church cathedral and the close relationship between the cathedral and St John's is in itself a potentially interesting study in interaction between religous communities in medieval Dublin. The only comparable material which was still extant when inventories of church records were made in the nineteenth century were the medieval deeds of the Dublin parishes of St Catherine & St James, St Werburgh and St Nicholas Within. These were destroyed in the fire in the Public Record Office of Ireland in 1922. However, one deed from the St Catherine's collection for the year 1309[9] has survived while the material from the St Catherine's and St Werburgh's collections survives, in part, in published calendars.[10]

Diocesan records have fared somewhat better although there is scarcely an embarrassment of riches. The most important collection, by far, is the seven registers of the archbishops of Armagh, beginning with that of Milo Sweteman in 1361 and ending with that of George Cromer in 1535.[11] Similar registers survive for the dioceses of Dublin (the thirteenth-century Crede Mihi[12] and the sixteenth-century Liber Alani Niger[13]), Ossory (the fourteenth-century Red Book of Ossory[14]) and Limerick (the fourteenth-century Black Book of Limerick).[15] The Armagh registers have been deposited in the Public Record Office in Belfast, the Black Book of Limerick is in the custody of the Roman Catholic diocesan authorities Limerick and the other registers are in the Representative Church Body Library. These episcopal registers are for the most part compilations of earlier documents, many of which no longer survive, which affected the rights and privileges of the bishop. They also include contemporary memoranda which would be necessary for the efficient administration of the diocese: papal bulls and royal grants confirming privileges and possessions; papers relating to appointments, resignations and the discipline of the clergy; leases and related documents concerning estates and advowsons (the right to nominate clergy to a parish). The Liber Niger Alani, for example, was compiled by Archbishop Alen in the sixteenth century but contains copies of documents from the twelfth century onwards. Also, almost inevitably, diocesan registers contain interpolations of rather more exotic material which have little direct bearing on episcopal administration but which can lend some colour to the interpretation of local events – the Red Book of Ossory, for example, includes the texts of some sixty songs composed in the first half of the fourteenth century by Bishop Richard Ledred for the vicars of St Canice's cathedral to sing at the great festivals so that their mouths 'be not defiled with theatrical, foul and secular songs'. The same volume also includes a treatise on aqua vitae; not, as might be supposed, whiskey, which was not distilled in Ireland until the sixteenth century, but brandy, which in the medieval world was deemed to have medicinal properties.

The profile of cathedral records is even more fragmentary than that of diocesan records. Only two cathedrals, St Patrick's and Christ Church, Dublin, have extant medieval archives. In the case of the former a few pre-Reformation deeds are supplemented by the Dignitas Decani, an early sixteenth-century register containing copies of deeds and related documents from the twelfth century[16], and by the Dublin Troper, a fourteenth-century liturgical manu-script with some early sixteenth-century administrative memoranda.[17] The Christ Church material is more extensive but not abundant. There are two surviving registers, the fourteenth-century Liber Niger and the sixteenth-century Liber Albus, which are administrative compilations similar in content to the episcopal registers[18] (that is, copies of documents relating to rights and privileges and contemporary administrative memoranda), fourteenth-century account rolls[19], some miscellaneous medieval memoranda, and three liturgical manuscripts – a thirteenth-century martyrology, a fourteenth-century psalter[20] and a fifteenth-century book of obits.[21] The last of these, the book of obits, is a particularly valuable source for identifying the members of the cathedral community and those from the wider world who chose to be associated with it. The Christ Church deeds were destroyed in 1922 but they survive in part in an eighteenth-century transcription[22] and as a printed calendar and are an exceedingly rich source of information on people and places from the twelfth century onwards, not only for the cathedral but also for the city and county of Dublin.[23] The medieval muniments of St Patrick's, apart from the Dublin Troper which is in the University Library in Cambridge, are in the Representative Church Body Library, as are those of Christ Church, with the exception of the book of obits and martyrology which are bound together in one volume in Trinity College Library, Dublin, and the psalter, which is in the Bodleian Library.

This small corpus of Irish medieval ecclesiastical archives which has survived may be usefully augmented by the records of the papacy and by the fragmentary administrative records of the Irish religious houses. Since Rome was the spiritual and administrative centre of the western church the papal

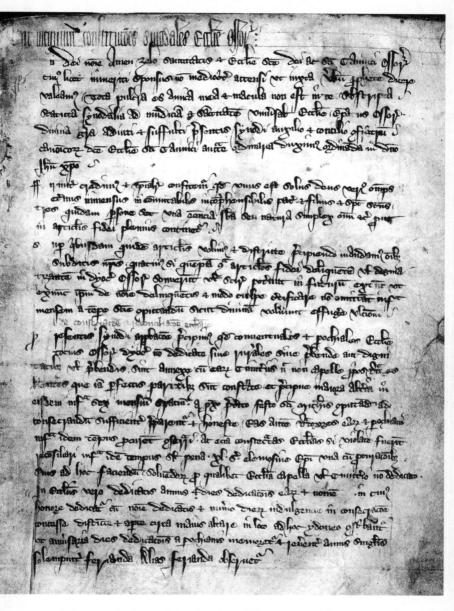

2. The constitutions of the diocese of Ossory, 6 October 1317,
from the Red Book of Ossory, a fourteenth century
diocesan register written in Latin
(R.C.B. Library D11/1/2, f.6)

archives inevitably contain much documentation about Irish parishes, dioceses, cathedrals, bishops and clergy with valuable information on the state of the church in localities throughout the country. This is most accessible through the on-going series of *Calendars of papal letters*, amounting so far to nineteen volumes, which covers the years 1198–1513[24] and from *Pontifica Hibernica* which contains papal chancery documents concerning Ireland for the years 640 to 1261.[25] In addition, registers of a number of Irish monastic foundations survived the dissolution of the monasteries which resulted in the destruction and scattering of the contents of their libraries, cloisters, presses and chests. The extent of the losses, although certainly substantial, cannot be quantified but a number of these manuscripts did survive: some were secreted and carried abroad into continental Europe, some were retained locally in lay custody, while others were gathered up by intellectuals and collectors such as James Ussher, archbishop of Armagh, whose manuscripts formed the basis of the collection in the Library of Trinity College, Dublin, and Sir James Ware of Castle Street in Dublin, many of whose manuscripts have ended up in the Bodleian Library in Oxford. In differing ways and at different periods much of this material has found its way into the great public collections of Ireland, Britain and continental Europe and the riches of the libraries of the Royal Irish Academy, Trinity College, Dublin, the British Library and others are ample testimony to this development.[26]

An invaluable supplement to the limited written record of the celtic and medieval Church is the evidence of architecture and archaeology. There may be no surviving archives for many of the once important monastic foundations, medieval cathedrals and their satellite churches but much physical evidence survives, above and below ground, and the work of the national and local heritage bodies has done much in recent years to bring this to light and to interpret it for a wider audience. Publications such as Peter Harbison's monumental work on Irish high crosses[27], Roger Stalley's seminal study of Cistercian architecture[28] and the survey of the medieval churches of County Offaly[29] provide a wealth of information on local sites and buildings, many of which may be visited. Indeed the portfolio of ecclesiastical buildings in the care of the Office of Public Works, and the easily accessible literature which is freely available about them, are astonishingly rich sources.

Because so few Irish ecclesiastical records have survived from the medieval period there is perhaps an understandable reluctance to engage in the study of local medieval ecclesiastical communities for fear that there is little new to discover. However, the Church was involved in virtually all aspects of human activity in medieval Ireland and so the judicious use of the extant records of central government, municipal corporations and charitable and fraternal bodies, together with the evidence of archaeology and architecture, as supplements to the surviving ecclesiastical sources offers a prospect of interesting and rewarding research opportunities.

II. THE CHURCH OF IRELAND 'AS BY LAW ESTABLISHED': FROM THE REFORMATION TO 1871

The Church of Ireland 'as by law established' was a product of the Reformation in the sixteenth century. Following Henry VIII's break with Rome, which was completed in 1534, the Church in Ireland ceased to be part of the universal catholic Church governed from Rome and became an arm of the English establishment in Ireland: in effect a part of the apparatus of government. A parliament of 1536 extended to Ireland the laws governing the Church which had already come into force in England. Thus Henry became the supreme head of the Church of Ireland and all office holders in the Church had to swear to that fact by taking the Oath of Supremacy. The diocesan or consistorial courts of the bishops continued to exercise a twofold jurisdiction inherited from the medieval Church. The voluntary jurisdiction included the granting of probates and administrations, sequestrations of livings, institutions and collations, licences for marriages, curates and school-masters, the granting of faculties for building and alterations to buildings, while the contentious jurisdiction included testamentary and matrimonial suits, tithe cases, causes of correction such as non-residence or immorality by clergy or defamation or adultary by the laity. However, appeals to Rome were forbidden. Yet these reforms had little effect on the day to day practice of religion which continued much as before so that the Henrician Reformation was spoken of as having produced 'Catholicism without the Pope'. One aspect of Henry's religious reforms, however, did have a marked effect – the sup-pression of the monasteries, which began in earnest in 1537. Most religious houses were suppressed and their property, both real and moveable, used to endow the crown and its supporters. However, some monasteries were spared and survived in a reformed fashion such as the Benedictine abbey in Downpatrick which became a diocesan cathedral, and the Augustinian foundation of Holy Trinity, Dublin which was transformed into the cathedral of Christ Church with the prior and members of the convent becoming a dean and chapter of secular clergy: other monastic churches were converted into parish churches.

Following the death of Henry VIII and the accession of Edward VI in 1547, the Church of Ireland, in imitation of its English counterpart, began to take on a more protestant character. The principal vehicle for this was the introduction in 1549 of the *Book of Common Prayer* which was to be used in all the churches of the country. This new service book not only provided a reformed liturgy but published it in English and thereafter English, rather than Latin, gradually became the administrative language of the Church of Ireland. After the brief Catholic respite of the reign of Queen Mary, Elizabeth returned the Church of Ireland to protestantism in 1561 with the re-enactment of the Act of Supremacy, by which she became chief governor of the Church, and the imposition of an Act of Uniformity which made compulsory attendance at church services using the *Book of Common Prayer.*

However, despite the reformation of the Irish church by the Tudor monarchs, the subsequent plantation of parts of Ireland by English and Scottish settlers, and the effects of the penal laws, the Church of Ireland remained a minority religion, but as the official church of the state it exercised a degree of influence and wielded an authority which was disproportionate to its numerical strength. Its parishes were units of local government, its courts were centres of matrimonial and testamentary jurisdiction, its prelates and clergy were often important officers of state, and its churches were for periods the only places in which acts of worship were permitted under the law. The laws which created the established Church were never uniformly applied but were nonetheless of sufficient significance to have created by the middle of the eighteenth century the fabric of the protestant ascendancy. Membership of the established Church was the key not alone to ecclesiastical advancement but to the attainment of public office and the ownership of land. Thus to the ranks of the Church of Ireland were attracted not only those who were convinced by its theology but many who, out of political, social or economic expediency, found it prudent to become, at least nominally, members of the established Church.

The administrative framework of the established Church was in essence not dissimilar to the pre-Reformation Church apart from the substitution of the crown for the pope. It retained parishes, dioceses with their bishops and cathedrals, and was governed at the top level by the government in the form of the monarch, his ministers and their administrative superstructure.[30] Parish life remained at the heart of the church for it was in the local communities that the faithful worshipped, experienced the Christian rites of passage, and ordered much of their social and economic life. The administrative structure of the parish was typically the clergy (a parish priest and perhaps a curate), two churchwardens, a parish clerk, a parish schoolmaster, and the vestries – select and general.

Then, as today, the clergy were the most important part of the parish administration. They were appointed to their parishes by whoever owned the advowson (the right of presentation to a church living), usually the bishop or the crown but, in some cases, a prominent local family. Their income came from tithes (a tax of ten per cent on crops, livestock and the fruits of labour), fees for pastoral services (baptisms, marriages and burials) and offerings. When the local clergyman was entitled to the whole tithes he was called a rector but the tithes could be appropriated to another ecclesiastical person or corporation or to a lay person. In such circumstances the owner of the tithes was obliged to provide a clergyman to fulfil the duties which the owner could not or would not undertake and such a clergyman was called a vicar (a deputy) who was paid a part of the tithes, the remainder, usually the greater part, being reserved to the owner. The principal duty of the clergy was the cure of souls,

3. The opening page of the register of the parish of St John the Evangelist, Dublin, 1619: the oldest extant parish register in Ireland (R.C.B. Library P328/1/1)

which apart from the celebration of the eucharist and the saying of the offices of morning and evening prayer, was essentially the baptism of children, the solemnization of marriages, and the burial of the dead. The records of this clerical activity are enshrined in the parish registers of baptisms, marriages and burials. Despite an attempt in 1617 to require clergy to keep registers and to make regular returns to a 'public register' in Dublin the earliest surviving Church of Ireland register, that for the parish of St John the Evangelist, Dublin, does not begin until 1619. Indeed until the promulgation of the 1634 Canons of the Irish Church there was no requirement to keep registers, unlike the situation in England where the 1538 Canons had made this obligatory. It is therefore scarcely surprising that only three parishes, all in Dublin, are known to have kept registers before 1634. The one fact which almost everyone knows about Church of Ireland parish registers is that they were all destroyed in the fire in the Public Record Office of Ireland in 1922. Like most *clichés* this is a simplification and only partly true. Records of some 1,006 parishes were destroyed in 1922, but the registers of 637 parishes were at that time held in local custody under retention orders and so survived, while of those registers which were destroyed many had been copied locally in whole or in part before deposit in the Public Record Office. In addition the registers of the important Dublin parishes of St Andrew and St Michan and the mid-seventeenth century register of the Liberties of Cashel had been published by the Parish Register Society of Dublin and so although the original registers were destroyed in 1922 all the information which they contained has survived.[31]

A valuable supplement to parish registers, particularly in parishes for which the registers have been destroyed, are gravestone and memorial inscriptions. Both frequently carry much more information than the names of deceased and the dates of death. Many have details of the extended family and information on places of residence and occupations while the more florid of them will include appreciations of the character of the deceased. In addition to the information which is inscribed on gravestones and memorials their size, decorative style and location in the church or churchyard may be useful guides to the wealth, sophistication and status of local families.[32] Inevitably many of the older graveyards are abandoned and overgrown and their investigation will require an unusual degree of preparation and persistence and a not inconsiderable amount of physical strength to clear undergrowth and, on occasions, to lift up stones which have fallen down. In the case of memorials and gravestones sited within churches, arrangements will have to be made with local custodians since most churches are locked outside the time of services. Although there has not been a systematic programme to record inscriptions much valuable work has been done and a good deal of this has been published.[33]

In those parish registers which survive, the amount of detail which they contain and, therefore, their usefulness for local studies, varies. The content of seventeenth and eighteenth-century registers is, for the most part, confined to the date of the event being recorded and the names of the parties involved with the only general exception to this being baptismal registers which include the names of the parents of the child. In the case of baptismal and burial registers these are exactly as their title indicates and not records of births and deaths, the dates of which have to be inferred. It is not until the nineteenth century, with the appearance of pro-forma registers, that more detail on individuals and families becomes commonplace: information such as ages, addresses, occupations, dates of birth and death, and often the causes of death. In the case of marriage registers, the inclusion of the names of witnesses, who were frequently members of the family, increases the usefulness of the records while the appearance of signatures allows some conclusions to be drawn about the spread of literacy. Registers can also reflect aspects of the lives of residents of a parish who were not members of the Church of Ireland. Presbyterian ministers were not permitted to conduct marriages until 1782 and could not perform 'mixed marriages' (marriages of a Presbyterian to a non-Presbyterian) before 1845 while Methodists could not conduct marriages until 1845 and did not begin to administer baptism until the 1830s: both denominations resorted to the Church of Ireland for these rites of passage. The same is true of burials for the Church of Ireland graveyard was frequently used as the burying place for the whole community, including Roman Catholics, although this practise is sometimes obscured by local varients of registration. In some parishes all burials are recorded in the Church of Ireland register and often the religion of the deceased, if not Church of Ireland, is noted but in other parishes it has been the practise to record only the Church of Ireland interments. However, whilst parish registers are invaluable sources for identifying and analysing local communities they are not always a complete chronicle of the community for they are only a record of the three principal Christian rites of passage. It is possible that people lived in a parish for the greater part of their lives and yet did not appear in the register of that parish: they may have been born elsewhere, they may have married, as was the custom from time immemorial, in the parish of the bride, and may have been buried in a family grave in another part of the country. For a fuller record of the local community, parish registers ought to be used in conjunction with vestry records.

The vestry (its name comes from the word for a room in which the priest kept his vestments and in which the local people met to discuss parish business) was the assembly of all the rate payers of the parish which, after the abolition of the penal laws, included all rate payers irrespective of their religion. This was the general vestry which levied a local tax or cess that paid for a range of local services such as street cleaning, poor relief, fire fighting and parish constables. The extent of these civil functions varied from place to place depending on the needs of the local population and the ability of local communities to finance those needs. Inevitably there was more activity in the cities and larger towns and especially in Dublin where the anglican presence was most pervasive. However, the Irish vestries were never as effective as their English counterparts and many local services were provided on a county basis by the grand juries. In addition to the general vestry there was a select vestry composed of rate paying protestants which levied modest taxes for the maintenance of the church buildings and the payment of parish officers. The churchwardens were the principal officers of the general vestry. Two wardens, who had to be protestants, were elected each year and their duties were to maintain order during services (the ceremonial wands which churchwardens still carry have, like civic maces, their origins in the need for a weapon to keep order), to represent the parish legally and to serve as the parish treasurers.[34]

The records of the vestries are among the richest sources for local and parish history and for the history of religion in Ireland. Vestry minute books record the civil and religious activities of the parish, the administrative decisions of the vestry and details of those responsible for taking those decisions. They may include lists of those who paid the parish cess and they may contain the annual financial statements of the church wardens, although in some parishes there are separate cess books and churchwardens' account books. Cess records are particularly useful for identifying local communities and estimating the relative status of the members of a community. They list the names of occupiers of houses in the parish, street by street, lane by lane, and so can offer, for example, the prospect of examining shifts in settlement patterns within parishes, while the sums of money for which each householder was assessed can give an impression of the relative wealth of individuals and of areas within a town or city. A greater breadth of financial information may be had from the churchwardens' accounts: expenditure on coal for widows, clothing for poor children and coffins for paupers can reveal much about the charitable dimension of parish life. An examination of the amounts of money which were spent on bread and wine may allow conclusions to be drawn about the frequency of celebrations of Holy Communion, while the church-wardens' accounts are often prime sources for information on the building, furnishing and maintenance of churches, schools and halls. At best, vestry records are an enormously valuable source of information on clergy, local families and their wealth and status, church buildings and exercise of religion, and what we now think of as local government services. The earliest surviving vestry book is from the parish of St John the Evangelist, Dublin and begins in 1595 while the earliest churchwardens' account book, apart from the medieval accounts of the parish of St Werburgh, Dublin, is from the Dublin parish of St Bride and begins in 1663. However, relatively few parishes have vestry records which pre-date the early years of the eighteenth century.

The value of vestry records as a source for identifying and analysing local communities, is complemented by the records of tithes which, like the parish cess, were a form of tax levied and recorded on a parish basis. Tithes, as a tax on crops, livestock and labour had been introduced during the reign of Henry II (1154–89) as a means of supporting the Church but they were not common outside the greater Dublin area until the reign of Elizabeth I (1558–1603) when they became a means of financing the established church. By the early eighteenth century two-thirds of the Church of Ireland's income came from rectorial tithes. Tithes were payable not only by members of the Church of Ireland but by Roman Catholics and dissenters and so the records of tithe applotment, or assessment, which were compiled in the 1820s are invaluable sources not only for estimating the wealth of Church of Ireland communities but also for analysing the compostion of the wider parish. Under the terms of an act of parliament of 1823, tithes could be paid in cash instead of kind, and the sums for which each tithe payer was liable were recorded in the tithe applotment book for each parish. These were compiled by parochial commissioners, one of whom was appointed by the Church of Ireland bishop and the other elected by the rate payers. The applotment books list not only the payment which was due to the owner of the tithes, but also the names of the occupiers of land and the quantity and quality of the land which they held. Some tithe applotment books have survived among parish record collections in the Representative Church Body Library but the principal collections are in the National Archives and, for the parishes of Northern Ireland, in the Public Record Office in Belfast.

Another category of parish record, which like the tithe applotment books, is nineteenth century in origin, is preachers' books. These volumes record the dates and types of services which were held in each church, the names of the officiating clergy, the amount of the offertory, the numbers in the congregation and, where appropriate, the numbers receiving Holy Communion. They are, therefore, invaluable records for estimating the health, both financial and spiritual, of a parish and are a useful supplementary source for determining the places in which clergy, particularly curates who might not otherwise be well documented, served. Furthermore they are frequently the only official record of the closure of a church as they record the date of the last service. Preachers' books have been little used by local historians, largely because of doubts about their statistical reliability, and there certainly have been instances in which it has been common practise to estimate, often generously, the size of the congregation rather than count the number of people present. However, preachers' books are often the only guide to the numbers who attended a church and so, despite reservations about their total integrity, they remain an important source for analysing local Church of Ireland communities. Another aspect of preachers' books, which can provide unexpected local colour and a somewhat capricious range of information and opinion is the comments column. Comments on the weather can often explain variations in church attendance, while the name of a charity or organization for which there was a special service may indicate a particular style of churchmanship or suggest, as in the case of support for overseas missions, an unusual degree of contact between a rural community and the Church in a foreign land. Comments on local events can be valuable as Peter Hart has demonstrated by using preachers' books in County Cork as a source for local outrages during the Civil War.[35] Such appreciation of the value of preachers' books is relatively new. Until recently they were regarded by most parish clergy as being of little significance and were frequently banished to obscure cupboards and out buildings where their survival was largely a matter of chance. Few such collections, however, fared as disastrously as the preachers' books of one Ulster parish: these for some inexplicable reason were lodged in the boot of the rector's car which was destroyed by fire in a local garage!

The nineteenth century, as well as being an era of increasing order in parish administration, was also an age of self improvement and wholesome recreation and the parish was often the focus of such activity. Debating societies, drama groups and lawn tennis clubs vied for parishioners' time with Sunday schools, temperance societies, local branches of organizations such as the Young People's Christian Endeavour Society and the Y.M.C.A.. This activity was resolutely minuted and its costs accounted for, and although the survival of such records is patchy, they can offer an additional dimension to the study of local Church of Ireland communities.

The survival rate of modern parish records has not been good. Inadequacies in record keeping were commonplace in Ireland; the unsettled state of the country, and in particular the effects of the 1641 Rebellion, the Cromwellian depradations, the Jacobite and Williamite wars and the 1798 Rebellion, militated against the systematic keeping of records, their safe storage and their transmission from one generation to another, while most catastrophic of all, the fire in the Public Record Office of Ireland in 1922 obliterated the parish collections which had been deposited there. The collections which survive are in the Representative Church Body Library, the National Archives and the Public Record Office in Belfast, although a significant number of parishes still retain custody of their own records.

Above the parishes in the pyramidal structure of the Church of Ireland were the dioceses. In the established Church the diocesan administration was, to all intents and purposes, the bishop and the officers whom he appointed to assist him in his administrative functions. Bishops were appointed by the crown and were, in effect, agents of the English administration in Ireland: therefore they were, for the most part, Englishmen or Irishmen who were sympathetic to the English interest in Ireland. Inevitably also the appointment of bishops was coloured by the current state of English politics and there was much letter writing and visits to London or Bath when there were episcopal vacancies. For most of the period of the established church there were four archbishoprics and twenty-two bishoprics. Of course some were more sought

At a vestry legally Summon'd and h[...] on Wednesday
the 22d Jan'y 1777 in the Parish Church of St Nicholas
for said parish. We the [Elec]tors, Churchwardens & parish-
-eners. Do agree that the following Sums of money be raised
and levied on the parishoners of sd parish for the use of
said Church & Church yard, and for the paym'. of said
Sums as shall be expended by the present Churchwardens

Sextons Sallary		£10
Sacrament Wine		3.10
D[itt]o Bread		0..9.9
Winding the Clock		5.5
Gen Ink Paper & making State books		1.2.9
Sand and Brushes		.7.9
to the Sexton for washing the Church Linnen		16.3
Visitation fees		6.8
Mrs Brittons bill.		19.10¼
Paid for cleaning the pipe of the Stoves		1.4
to Mr Rich'd Bird for Repairing ye Church Windows		15
Repairing the Church Roof		11.6
Deficiency in ye collection appointed the 11 Jan'y 1776		3
for a new Flew for one of the Stoves		3.9
[...] for 6 Barrels of coals		1.7
for improvem'. & repairs of the C yard		10..19.1
		£38.1.4¼

Alex: Lamilliere, Minister.

James Norman   John Good   } C. Wardens
    Tho: Alleyn

Geo: Fuller
John Touchstone
Will Clerks
Rich'd Burt

4. Minutes of a meeting of the vestry of the parish of St Nicholas,
Cork, 22 January 1777 (R.C.B. Library P498/5/1)

after than others, in particular the archbishoprics of Armagh, Dublin, Cashel and Tuam, in that order, and the bishopric of Derry, and there were frequent translations (that is, internal promotions of bishops) as the holders of Irish bishoprics sought a more prestigious and better endowed appointment. That is not to say that all the Irish bishops were cynical place seekers (although many were) but in an age when there was no clear distinction between civil and religious order, patronage and factionalism were an accepted part of the system.

Episcopal correspondence tended to be treated as the private property of bishops rather than church archives and many collections are to be found in national and local repositories in Britain and Ireland rather than among the diocesan archives. Since many of the bishops were English their correspondence is often to be found among the papers of their families in county record offices or the British Library. For example Charles Broderick, archbishop of Cashel from 1801 to 1822, was a member of the Midleton family and his papers are with those of the earls of Midleton in Surrey County Record Office while William Stuart, archbishop of Armagh from 1800 to 1822 was the son of the earl of Bute and his correspondence is to be found with that of his family in the Bedfordshire Record Office. Those collections which remained in Ireland tended to gravitate towards the Library of Trinity College, Dublin since the Church of Ireland did not have its own library until the 1930s[36], but for many of the bishops no personal archive is known to survive in any repository, which is scarcely surprising since many were far from distinguished. However, even if many bishops did not generate or preserve their own archive something of their activity at a diocesan or national level may often be discerned from the national political and religious collections in England. Church of Ireland bishops were part of the English administration in Ireland and so were frequently written to by government ministers and their functionaries in London and these transactions are preserved in the Public Record Office in London, in the State Papers, Ireland and the Home Office Papers, Ireland series.[37] Furthermore, the Irish bishops and especially the archbishops corresponded with their counterparts in England and the archives of the archbishops of Canterbury, in Lambeth Palace Library, London, and, to a lesser extent, those of the archbishops of York, in the Borthwick Institute of Historical Research in York, may be useful sources.

The principal functions of the bishops were to ordain and confirm and to visit their dioceses and in fulfilment of these duties they appointed clergy and parish officers, and could discipline those whom they had appointed. The ordinations of clergy and the appointment of parish officers were entered on subscription rolls. These rolls of parchment recorded the nature and date of the appointment and contained the signature of the appointee and were prefaced by the subscriptions or oaths which the appointees made: they subscribed to the Act of Supremacy, the Act of Uniformity and declared their opposition to transubstantiation. Appointments of clergy to parishes and the licencing of curates and parishes officers were recorded in diocesan registers (sometimes also called title books) which also included records of other episcopal acts such as the consecration of a new church or graveyard. Potentially the most labour intensive episcopal activity was visitation when the diocesan cathedral and all the parishes in the diocese would be inspected by the bishop to determine the physical condition of the buildings, the effectiveness of the clergy and the fidelity of the laity. In well-run dioceses this was a frequent event and the visitation books which resulted therefrom provide invaluable snapshots of the diocese at particular times. Bishop Isaac Mann's visitation of the diocese of Cork in 1781 recorded the names of the benefices and the clergy (rectors, vicars and curates) who served them and where they resided; the physical condition of the churches; the size of the glebe; the name of the patron of the living; and the names of the parish clerks, schoolmasters, church-wardens and sidesmen. He noted, among other things, that Templemichael church was in ruins, while in Cork the church of St Paul was in repair but the walls of St Peter's were in danger of falling in, and the rector of Leighmoney was found to have lived four miles away in Bandon while the rector of Inchigeelagh was only one of six parochial clergy to reside in a glebe house.[38] Not every function was carried out by the bishop personally: the vicar-general acted as a surrogate or deputy and frequently took the place of the bishop at visitations, in signing licences and in presiding at the diocesan court in which wills were proved, marriage licences issued, and clergy and laity disciplined. In addition the diocesan registrar prepared documents, was in charge of the registry and was, in effect, the diocesan archivist.

In the registry, as well as the subscription rolls, title books and visitation returns were the records of the consistorial court, especially probated wills, administrations of estates of those who had died intestate, marriage licences and marriage licence bonds, and papers relating to disciplinary proceedures, particularly against clergy. Following the Henrician Reformation appeals to Rome were forbidden and jurisdiction in such matters was transferred to the prerogative court of the archbishop of Canterbury and, during the reign of Elizabeth I, these responsibilites were vested in the prerogative court of the Archbishop of Armagh. Similar courts operated at diocesan level with each bishop presiding in person or by surrogate in his consistorial court. Wills were proved and estates administered in the appropriate diocesan court unless the estate of the deceased had a value of £5 or more in another diocese, in which case probate or administration was granted by the prerogative court. In consequence of this activity a huge body of testamentary material of value to historians and genealogists accumulated in the diocesan registeries. In particular, the collections of wills and administrations contained much detail about local families and their wealth and property and, in the cases of wills which were proved in the prerogative court, their relationships with the wider world. However, in 1858 the Probate Act removed this testamentary jurisdiction from the Church of Ireland and the wills which had been filed in the consistorial courts were transferred to the Public Record Office of Ireland where they were largely destroyed by fire in 1922.[39] However, a considerable amount of the information which was lost in 1922 has survived in printed form[40] or has been recovered from the collections of families, solicitors and genealogists[41].

Matrimonial jurisdiction was also exercised by the diocesan courts for until the late-eighteenth century a marriage had to be conducted by Church of Ireland clergy in order to be legally valid. Those intending to marry in the Church of Ireland had to preface this event with the 'calling of the banns' in the parish churches of those who were to be married.[42] This provided an opportunity for those who believed the intended marriage to be unlawful to object. An alternative method of proceeding was to obtain a marriage licence from the bishop but this option also involved indemnifying the diocesan author- ities, by means of a marriage licence bond, against prosecution for authorising an invalid marriage. Matrimonial disputes also came before the consistorial courts and the records of such disputes, together with the licences and bonds, formed an immensely important archive of information on local families and their interaction with families outside their dioceses. As a consequence of the disestablishment of the Church of Ireland the Church's matrimonial juris- diction was abolished and the records of this activity were transferred to the Public Record Office of Ireland where like the testamentary records, they were largely destroyed in 1922. However, indexes to marriage licence bonds and some abstracts[43] have survived and some of these have been published.[44]

The scenario is similar with matters of discipline. The records of the ecclesiastical courts were also destroyed in 1922 and the fragmentary material which has survived by way of stray records and abstracts[45] can only hint at the wealth of information, much of it intensely local in its orientation, which was lost. For example, a series of depositions in the case against Thomas Ward, dean of Connor, who was deprived of his office for adultery, drunkness and non-residence, provides graphic evidence of local life from every day people in Carrickfergus and Lisburn in the late seventeenth century.[46] The same is also broadly true of the records of the episcopal estates which were also stored in the diocesan registries. The activities of the bishops were largely funded from the receipts of landed estates, which were part of the diocesan endow- ment, and their administration produced maps, rentals, rent rolls and tithe records. These archives not only reflected aspects of episcopal organization but also detailed much of the lives of the bishops' tenants at different levels of society. Only the dioceses of Armagh and Dublin have significant extant estate collec- tions while there are fragmentary survivals for Ossory, Killaloe, and Cloyne. However, the records in the Registry of Deeds, Dublin, in which land trans- actions from 1708 are registered, and the private papers of families who were episcopal tenants, allow the recovery of the some information from this source.

	£	s	d
to mr Pease for keeping the organs	02	00	00
to the Beadle a yeares sallary & lodgeing	03	00	00
to the Scavinger a yeares sallary	02	00	00
for Cleaning ye marble at ye Comunion table	00	07	06
The Provsts Allowance	12	00	00
Totall ordinary Disbursmts	233	09	10
Extraordinary Disbursmts			
for 2 doz: of prickers	00	08	00
for Scouring ye Branch twice & mending it	00	05	06
To the vicars the 5th of Nov: p ordr	01	00	00
to the upholsterer for the seat of the officer of the Traine	00	13	06
to a guard on Alderman Quins Body p order	00	06	00
to Davys slator p bill	19	19	06
to two laborers in the Church	00	02	00
for silver weights	00	06	00
to the Smith p bill	01	01	10
to John Powell p bill	01	09	03
to the Coroner for inquest in 1671 p ordr	00	13	04
to, Hoatly slator p bill	05	00	02
more to him p bill	19	01	02
more to him	05	00	00
more to him p bill	02	14	03
to the Plumer p bill	17	09	04½
for a Gowne for the virger	02	10	00

5. Extract from the proctors' accounts of Christ Church cathedral,
Dublin, showing examples of ordinary and extraordinary
disbursements, 1675–5 (R.C.B. Library C6/1/15/1)

The other part of the diocesan hierarchy was the cathedral in which the bishop had his throne and in which, by tradition, he preached and celebrated the eucharist at Christmas and Easter. Following the Henrician Reformation all cathedrals became ecclesiastical corporations of secular clergy, that is they were separate entities under the law and able to hold property in common for a particular purpose, with a typical cathedral chapter consisting of a dean, precentor, chancellor, treasurer and a variable number of canons. In addition, the vicars choral, the professional core of the choir, might be a separate ecclesiastical corporation with its own endowments. Furthermore there were a number of functionaries who were employees of the cathedral: organists, vergers, sextons, pew-openers and so on. The work of the cathedral revolved around the sung services (matins and evensong daily and the eucharist on Sundays and on feast days) and this *opus Dei*, and the work of administering and financing it, is reflected in the cathedral archives which were the responsibility of the chancellor. The meetings of the chapter were recorded by the chapter clerk, often a canon and invariably someone with legal training, in the chapter act books and the accounts were the responsibility of a proctor who was a member of the chapter elected annually and who produced an annual financial statement to justify his stewardship. The estates, which provided the revenues to maintain the building, the canons, and the administrative staff, were sometimes farmed out to stewards or senechals who commissioned maps and maintained rentals and rent rolls; the music and the records of choir attendance were usually the responsibility of two of the vicars choral appointed for those purposes. In addition there may be registers of baptisms, marriages and burials; building records and architectural drawings; deeds and lease books; and various miscellaneous papers which can on occasion usefully complement the principal series of documents in the cathedral archives.

The diocesan structures which are outlined above are, of course, ideal, and in reality varied greatly throughout the country depending on the strength of the local Church of Ireland community. Furthermore, and more importantly for our immediate purposes, the diocesan and cathedral archives of the Church of Ireland were, as we have seen, decimated by the fire in the Public Record Office of Ireland in 1922. Only the dioceses of Armagh, Dublin (including Glendalough and Kildare which were united to it), Ossory and Tuam have significant pre-disestablishment archives: the Armagh collection is in the Public Record Office in Belfast and the other collections are in the Representative Church Body Library. In the case of cathedrals there are only three substantial collections, namely those of Christ Church and St Patrick's, Dublin and St Canice's, Kilkenny, although there are fragmentary collections for Cork[47], Cloyne[48] and Kildare[49] dating from the seventeenth century, all of which, Cork apart, are in the Representative Church Body Library.

The situation is somewhat better at the top of the pyramid for although the records of central government in Ireland were also destroyed in 1922 the administrative records of England have survived and so among the public records in London there is much to be learnt about the administration of the Church of Ireland by the bishops and the ministers of state acting on behalf of the crown.[50] A particularly important agency of the government in Church affairs was the Board of First Fruits. First fruits or annates were the first year's revenue of a benefice, dignity or bishopric and before the Henrician Reformation they were remitted to Rome. Thereafter, this tax was paid to the crown but in 1711 it was transferred to a Board of First Fruits in Dublin which was given authority to use the money to buy up impropriations, aid the building and repair of churches, and to assist in the purchase and building of glebe houses. This was an initiative which changed the landscape of Ireland for the availablilty of funds led to an explosion of church building as churches which had been in ruins were repaired or more often replaced in whole or in part. Many churches bear the tell-tale marks of Board of First Fruits intervention having retained only a period tower to which has been added a relatively undistinguished barn-like structure in the place of the former nave and transepts. An even more telling hallmark of the work of the Board is the existence of the ruins of a medieval or early modern church close by an eighteenth or early nineteenth-century Board of First Fruits building. Perhaps the most striking example of this is in Thomastown, County Kilkenny, where the ruin and the replacement are literally side by side. Rather more distinguished was the role of the Board in facilitating the acquistion or commissioning of glebe houses and thereby many fine eighteenth and nineteenth-century country houses became Church of Ireland rectories. The records of the Board of First Fruits ought to be one of the most important sources for the history of architecture and building in Ireland but, alas, they too perished in 1922. However, a certain amount of the information is available in copy and extract form in different collections and while Hayes's *Manuscript sources* can assist in identifying some of these sources a patient trawl through the lists and indexes in the various repositories may be ultimately more rewarding. More conveniently, the entries in Lewis's *Topographical Dictionary*[51] and in the third and fourth report of the Irish Church Temporalities Commissioners[52] frequently cite the amounts of money which the Board made available to individual parishes, by way of grants and loans, to improve churches and encourage the provision of glebe houses.

The prime sources for information on the architectural heritage of the Church of Ireland have not survived well. Most of the building records and architectural drawings of churches and rectories were destroyed in the fire in the Public Record Office of Ireland in 1922 either because they were among the contents of the diocesan registries or were part of the archives of the Board of First Fruits, Church Temporalities Commissioners or Ecclesiastical Commissioners. Some building accounts do survive among parish and cathedral records: for example the records of the demolition and re-building St Werburgh's church, Dublin, in the eighteenth century[53]; the records of the restoration of Kildare Cathedral which began in the 1870s[54]; and the drawings of the distinguished architect, William Burgess, for the building of St Fin Barre's Cathedral in Cork[55]. There are also small collections of architectural drawings (ground plans, sections and, perhaps most usefully of all, elevations) of churches and rectories among some of the surviving diocesan collections, notably some fine drawings by John Semple of churches, mostly in the greater Dublin area, in the 1820s and 1830s[56], and some colourful elevations of churches and rectories in the west of Ireland.[57] More substantial is a large collections of drawings which has survived among the records of the Representative Church Body and which may have strayed from the collections of the Ecclesiastical Commissioners.[58] In addition, for those who are interested in the local architectural dimension of the Church of Ireland, the collections of the Irish Architectural Archive in Dublin are likely to be most useful while the files of the *Irish Builder*, which was the leading architectural journal of the late nineteenth and early twentieth century, contain many drawings and descriptions of Church of Ireland edifices both in a contemporary and historical context.

A related and equally elusive visual source is maps. Most of the Church of Ireland map collections were destroyed in the fire in the Public Record Office in 1922. There is no comprehensive and authoritative books of maps of the boundaries of the parishes and dioceses, although occasional maps survive among parish and diocesan collections and among the records of the Representative Church Body. The most important collection is that of the estates of the archbishop of Dublin. This relates mostly to lands in the city of Dublin and Counties Dublin and Wicklow, although there are some items from Counties Cork and Westmeath, and covers the period 1654 to 1850.[59] There are also useful collections for the dioceses of Armagh and Clogher from the mid-seventeeth century to the early twentieth century[60], and small miscellaneous collections for Christ Church[61] and St Patrick's cathedral, Dublin, mostly from the eighteenth and nineteenth centuries.[62]

The structure of the established Church survived, largely intact, until the early nineteenth century when, in the face of changing attitudes in Irish society, the Church of Ireland also had to change. The abolition of the penal laws in the late eighteenth century and the winning of Catholic emancipation in 1829 forced on the government the realization that the privileged position enjoyed by the Church of Ireland as the Church of only one eighth of the population could not be sustained. A Church Temporalities Act of 1833 abolished the archbishoprics of Cashel and Tuam, suppresssed ten other bishoprics, abolished the Board of First Fruits and established the Ecclesiastical Commissioners who were charged with using the moneys which were saved by these reforms to build and repair churches and improve the income of clergy in small parishes. The work of the Church Temporalities Commissioners is enshrined in four printed goverment reports which provide much valuable detail on the state of the Church of Ireland at parish and diocesan level in the early nineteenth century. The first report deals with the revenues and patronage of the bishops and includes the names of the lessees and tenants on the episcopal estates; the second is a similar digest of information for the deans and dignitaries of cathedrals; whilst the third and fourth reports provide a mass of detail on parishes – their patrons, clergy, officers, population, extent, churches, rectories, glebe lands, and income[63]. Many of the archives of the Church Temporalties Commissioners and the Ecclesiastical Commissioners were destroyed in 1922 but much remains in the National Archives, the Public Record Office of Northern Ireland and in the Representative Church Body Library.

The Irish Church Temporalities Act was a watershed in the administrative history of the Church of Ireland for it was the first time that government had intervened so directly in the affairs of the established Church. Its repercussions were felt both in England, where reaction to the act was the catalyst which led to the emergence of the Oxford Movement, and in Ireland where once the force of reform had gathered pace it could not be stopped. In 1838 the hated tithes were all but abolished. In 1845 civil registration of protestant marriages was introduced by which the Church of Ireland became simply a registration agent for the state with the registers supplied by the government and their contents collated in the General Register Office in Dublin. In 1857 the Probate Act removed the testamentary jurisdiction of church courts and transferred the collections of wills, probates and administrations to the Court of Probate. More importantly, however, the stage was set for the complete severing of the links between Church and state by the disestablishment of the Church of Ireland.

III. THE CHURCH OF IRELAND AS A VOLUNTARY CHRISTIAN COMMUNITY: FROM 1871 TO THE PRESENT

The Church of Ireland was disestablished by the Irish Church Act of 1869 which came into force on 1 January 1871. Under the terms of the act the Church was left with the cathedrals, churches and schools then in use but all other church lands and properties were vested in the Church Temporalities Commissioners who realised these assets and distributed the money to charitable and educational bodies including Maynooth College and the Presbyterian Church. The Church of Ireland was left with the clergy and bishops and a sum of about eight million pounds to fund them and was free to establish such structures as it thought appropriate for its new condition.[64]

The administrative structures which it devised were representative in nature and parliamentary in style. A General Synod was created which would be the Church's parliament in which the supreme authority would reside. Its membership was composed of two houses: the House of Bishops and the

House of Representatives, the latter consisting of clergy and laity from each of the dioceses with two lay members for each cleric. The members of the House of Representatives were elected by diocesan synods, which were local versions of the General Synod, and the members of the diocesan synods were elected by the parish vestries. The General Synod met annually, and a Standing Committee, composed of the bishops and two lay and two clerical members from each diocese, conducted business during the year. A similar system obtained in the dioceses with the diocesan synod being an annual assembly and a diocesan council conducting the business throughout the year. The administration of the temporalities of the disestablished Church was the function of the Representative Church Body which was created by the Irish Church Act as a perpetual trustee to take over such moneys and real and moveable property as was left with the Church of Ireland. It too, as its name implies, was representative in composition, with the bishops being joined by one cleric and two laymen from each diocese.

Apart from the creation of the General Synod, its diocesan equivalent and the Representative Church Body, the administrative apparatus of the Church seemed little changed by disestablishment. The parishes and the dioceses continued to be the principal administrative units and the bishops remained an an élite cadre of administrative officers. But if the structures remained much the same, the way in which they worked changed for a key component of disestablishment was the introduction of the idea of accountability, even if it was not overtly expressed. For the first time in its history the administration of the Church of Ireland from parish level up to the General Synod was account-able to the wider Church through the process of election. In the parishes the select vestries were elected each year while members of diocesan synods and councils, the General Synod and the Representative Church Body were elected triennielly. Another manifestation of this process of accountability was the production of annual reports by the principal administrative bodies of the Church, at central and local level, and the by host of subcommittees and fixed term commissions to examine particular issues, which they spawned. The model for this reporting procedure was the *Journal of the General Synod* which was not, as the title might suggest, simply the minutes of the annual meeting of the Synod, although it was that, but more importantly it was also a collection of reports from the various committees and commissions of the Church on their work over the preceeding year. The first General Synod *Journal* appeared in 1871 and has been published annually ever since and ought to be the starting point for any examination of the disestablished Church of Ireland. Similar annual reports were produced at diocesan and parish level and are usually to be found among the diocesan and parish archives.

However, like most annual reports the *Journal* and its local equivalents are compendia of information and the serious researcher will find only a part of the truth therein. The records of the parishes, cathedrals and dioceses continue to be important archival sources for the history of the Church as do those concerning the activities of the clergy and the bishops. The clergy, of course were absolved from the post disestablishment idea of election and, by extension did not have to report on their activities but they were responsible to their bishops who could discipline them if appropriate through the diocesan courts or the Court of the General Synod.[65] The bishops, however, although elected, initially by diocesan synods and more recently by electoral colleges, remained unaccountable and have steadfastly refused to become so. Despite their corporate identity as a house of the General Synod and their propensity to meet regularly they do not report to the General Synod on their activities. If they vote as a house at the Synod, as they did recently on the issue of the ordination of women, they vote in secret, whereas other members of the Synod, lay and clerical, vote in public, and they have refused to allow their records to be appraised much less be made available for researchers.

The major archival consequence of disestablishment was the decimation of the archives of the Church of Ireland. As a result of the Irish Church Act the records of the Church, which had hitherto been part of the establishment and, in effect, public records, became the property of a private civil organization. Concern arose about, in particular, the safety of parish registers, which for the period before civil registration of births, marriages and deaths[66], were the official records of such activity. The concern was not altruistic but arose from the need to protect information which was essential to establish family relationships and which therefore could affect rights of inheritance. The government legislated in 1875 to bring back into public ownership any Church of Ireland records which related to baptisms, marriages, burials or ordinations and all such records were to be transferred to the Public Record Office in Dublin. However, this legislation was subsequently amended so that only volumes containing records of baptisms and burials up to the end of 1870 and marriages up to the end of March 1845 came under the terms of the act, and if parishes could show that they could adequately care for their registers (in effect, could store them in a fireproof safe) they could retain them in local custody. However, despite the amended legislation many parishes, as we have already noted, deposited their registers in the Public Record Office in Dublin where they were destroyed in 1922. The records of the dioceses and cathedrals were similarly affected by disestablishment, for in preparation for the Irish Church Act, the Church Temporalities Commissioners largely emptied the diocesan registries and cathedral muniment rooms in their search for evidence of the church's wealth. When their work was completed the records were not returned to the Church but were transferred to the Public Record Office with the same catastrophic consequences as for the parish registers. Furthermore the Irish Church Act ended the residual jurisdiction of the ecclesiastical courts in matrimonial matters and transferred the records (marriage licences, marriage licence bonds and related material) to the registry of the Court for Matrimonial Causes from where they passed to the Public Record Office where they too perished in 1922.[67]

There was, however, a positive side to the events of 1922 for the destruction of so many ecclesiastical archives forced the Church of Ireland, for the first time, to give some consideration to this aspect of its corporate life. The result was the creation of an Ecclesiastical Records Committee in 1926 which set out initially to recover as much as it could of the information which had been lost in 1922. Copies of and extracts from destroyed records were collected; transcripts, calendars and lists were made of existing records; and from there it was but a short step to taking custody of archives which could not be adequately cared for in their original parish, cathedral or diocesan custody. Independently of this activity the Church of Ireland had opened its own Library, the Representative Church Body Library, in 1932 and in 1939 the functions of the Library and the Ecclesiastical Records Committee were amalgamated thereby creating the role of the Representative Church Body Library as the Church of Ireland's repository for its archives and manuscripts. As well as providing a home for the archives of the Church of Ireland the Library has developed as a focus for the personal papers of clergy and laity and the records of organizations and societies, dealing with education, mission, charity and recreation, which although closely associated with the Church of Ireland are not constitutionally part of it.[68]

The loss of many of the Church's archives in 1922 gave an enhanced importance to the work of researchers and scholars who had used these sources before their destruction. In particular the work of Canon J.B. Leslie and a small number of contemporaries and predecessors has ensured for posterity an immense body of biographical information on the clergy.[69] These 'biographical succession lists', as Leslie termed them, are pen portraits of clergy with details not only of their education and careers but also including, where possible, information on their antecedents and descendants. Notes of significant events in the life of the parishes and diocese in which the clergy served make this an additionally valuable source for the local researcher. Succession lists were compiled for the clergy of each diocese and within each volume there are sections on the bishops, cathedral chapters and parochial clergy with, on occasion, notes on parochial and diocesan history. Leslie produced succession lists for all the Irish dioceses except Cashel and Emly[70], Cork, Cloyne and Ross[71], Dromore[72], and Waterford and Lismore[73], for which successions had been published or were underway before he began his work, and whilst a number of Leslie's lists were printed[74] many remain unpublished as does his four volume index to all the succession lists.[75]

The archives and manuscripts of the Church are complemented by two invaluable primary printed sources, the *Church of Ireland Gazette* and the *Church of Ireland Directory*. The *Gazette*, which is the longest running weekly Church newspaper in Great Britain and Ireland, began its existence in 1856 as the *Irish Ecclesiastical Gazette* and changed to its present title in 1900. It is a kalidoscope of ecclesiastical information containing reports and comments on a wide variety of issues which absorbed the Church of Ireland, both nationally and locally, publishing the texts of sermons and addresses, reviewing books, and advertising an astonishing range of activities and services. Most valuable perhaps for the local historian is the section in each issue, quaintly entitled 'Diocesan Intelligence' which contained short accounts of local events in each diocese: the consecration of a church, the appointment of clergy, the installation of stained glass windows or the erection of memorials. Often the *Gazette* is the only source for dating such events. There is a complete run of the *Gazette* in the Representative Church Body Library together with typescript indexes. The most obvious limitation of the *Gazette* is that it does not begin until 1856. However, two other publications, the *Christian Examiner*, which began publication in 1825, and the *Irish Ecclesiastical Journal*, which appeared first in 1840, can provide valuable snippets of information on local Church of Ireland activity for earlier in the nineteenth century. The *Church of Ireland Directory* began in 1862 as *The Irish Church Directory* and changed to its present title only in 1967. It provided, for the first time, an annual list of clergy with details of their university degrees, dates of ordination and institution together with details of the benefices which they held, the size and value of the glebe, the numbers of worshipers who could be accommodated in the church and the name of the patron of the living. In addition the *Directory* carried a variety of supplementary details on diocesan officers and on Church of Ireland schools and voluntary organizations. There had been earlier Church of Ireland directories but they were occasional publications[76] rather than annuals while Irish clergy were not included in that great compendium of British clergy, *Crockford's Clerical Directory*, until 1883.

In 1967 the *Directory* introduced photographs of bishops and if this was the first occasion on which the Church of Ireland officially illustrated its prelates in such a way, it was no more than a public recognition of an activity which had been going on since the late sixteenth century. The acquisition and commissioning of portraits, mainly of bishops, but also in some places of deans, and often from the leading artists of the day, has created a substantial collection of colourful images of the leading churchmen of the last four centuries which are now to be found in episcopal residences, cathedrals and synod halls throughout the country.[77] The development of photography in the nineteenth century allowed the images of lesser clergy to be inexpensively recorded and many vestries are decorated with photographs of the rectors and curates who served in the parochial ministry. Taken together, the Church's collection of portraits and photographs of bishops and clergy, with their capacity to lend colour, both literally and metaphorically, to local studies, is an enormously valuable resource. Church of Ireland figures, both lay and clerical, were prominent also in the affairs of other leading Irish institutions and the portrait collections of organizations such as Dublin Corporation, Trinity College, Dublin and the King's Inns are likely to contain useful material as are the more important public gallery collections in Dublin, Belfast and Cork.

Finally, a source which is neither manuscript nor printed, and which to date has been little used, is the Church's large collection of plate. Chalices, patens, flagons, alms dishes, collecting plates, mostly in silver but also in silver gilt and silver plate, and frequently the work of leading Dublin and provincial silversmiths, were, more often than not, commemorative pieces. They were given or commissioned to mark the opening of a new church, to celebrate the fidelity of local clergy, to memorialize bishops and clergy, to give thanks for the birth of a child or to remember the life of a faithful member of a parish. As such they are often inscribed with genealogical and topographical information which can add much to local studies while their worth as artistic objects and their significance as pieces of church furniture can testify eloquently to the wealth, vibrancy, and sophistication of local communities and their leaders.

Access to the archives and manuscripts of the Church of Ireland

I. INTELLECTUAL ACCESS: HISTORIES, CATALOGUES AND EDITIONS

As in any form of original research, the successful use of Church of Ireland archives and manuscripts in local history projects will be enhanced and the research greatly facilitated by consulting the available printed sources before tackling the manuscript material. All researchers should familiarise themselves with the outline of the history and administration of the Church of Ireland, consult any published catalogues and lists of archives and manuscripts, and, where possible, use published editions of documents in the first instance. Much, if not all of this work can be done in any self-respecting reference library thus saving time and money which might be involved in travelling to the various repositories in which Church of Ireland material is to be found.

The most accessible history of the Church of Ireland is Kenneth Milne's short history, the most recent edition of which brings the story up to 1990.[1] R.B. MacCarthy's history, while equally brief, is somewhat idiosyncratic, although its origins, as a set of lectures given in Kilkenny with local examples, may make it particularly apposite reading for those whose research is centred on that area.[2] The standard academic history remains the three volume multi-authored study which was edited by Alison Phillips in 1933.[3] However, Milne's history, in particular, provides a balanced and measured overview of the development of the Church of Ireland from St Patrick to the present and the short time required to read it will equip the researcher with a context in which to better understand the locality in which he or she proposes to work. It might also be useful, although perhaps not essential in the initial stages of research, to look at one of the guides to the administration of the church. D.H. Akenson's chapter entitled 'The Eighteenth Century Church as an Administrative System'[4] is a useful introduction while for the Church today the most up to date work is Deane's *Church of Ireland handbook*, although Gilbert Wilson's earlier work has a useful administrative chart.[5] Many will find these to be valuable at the beginning of their research although others may prefer to use them as reference works as they proceed. At a more local level there are a number of diocesan and cathedral histories and a proliferation of publications relating to individual parishes. These vary considerably in size, scope and quality ranging from brief commemorative booklets to full-scale academic studies. However, even the most limited of them can provide a useful local chronology and context while the best are invaluable sources often containing local information, sometimes from oral sources, which is unavailable elsewhere. Older parish histories, especially those published at the end of the nineteenth century, frequently include long transcripts of parish records, especially protracted extracts from registers and vestry books, and these assume an added significance in the context of parishes for which the records have been destroyed subsequently. *The Irish Builder*[6] likewise included excerpts from parish records: for example, in the volume for 1886 there is an extended history of the parish of St Audeon, Dublin, including lengthy quotations from the vestry minute books, the originals of which have been missing for many years, and a running series on the churches of County Laois. The largest and most accessible collections of Church of Ireland parish histories is in the Representative Church Body Library.[7]

Published calendars, lists, indexes and descriptive articles on Church of Ireland archives and manuscripts do not abound but if there are relatively few specific publications, enough general catalogues and directories have appeared to give researchers an introduction to the topic with the minimum of effort. Pre-eminent in this regard is the multi-volume *Manuscript sources for the history of Irish civilization* and its three volume *Supplement*[8]. These comprise brief catalogue entries for archives and manuscripts relating to Ireland which are located in repositories not only in Ireland but throughout the world. The entries are arranged thematically with separate volumes for subjects, dates, places, persons and repositories. As well as describing the material, the catalogue entries include a location guide, which in the case of overseas material, is often a microfilm number from the National Library of Ireland whose extensive microfilming programme has made much, otherwise inaccessible material, readily available in Dublin. So, for example, by looking in the subject volume under the heading of visitations, a researcher can readily identify which dioceses have extant visitation books, for which period, and where they may be consulted. On a broader front one can look under the subject of Church of Ireland, which in turn is sub-divided into ten categories (benefices, clergy, controversy, conversions, convocation, disestablishment, liturgy, missions, property and revenue, general and miscellaneous) and obtain a general impression of the types of manuscript sources which are available.

However, *Manuscript sources* was published in 1965 and the *Supplement* in 1979 and, as much has happened in Church of Ireland archival circles since then, these volumes should be used in conjunction with more recent listings. Such a source is the National Register of Archives in London which each year solicits lists and indexes of archives and manuscripts, both published and unpublished, from British and Irish repositories. A master index allows researchers to quickly discover if there is relevant material among the lists and this facility is now available on the internet.[9] The National Library, Trinity

College, Dublin, the Public Record Office of Northern Ireland and the Representative Church Body Library regularly send material to the National Register and other Irish repositories have also contributed from time to time. Periodic digests of these contributions are published in *Irish Historical Studies*. However, the National Register operates a cut-off date of 1922 for Irish material and so is of limited significance for those engaged in twentieth-century studies. The National Register of Archives is a part of the Royal Commission on Historical Manuscripts, which since its foundation in 1869, has been surveying important collections of manuscripts and publishing the results of these exercises. Before Irish independence the writ of the Commission also ran in Ireland and many important Irish archives, including some Church of Ireland collections, were surveyed. These included the archives of the dioceses of Dublin and Ossory which were described by John Gilbert in the Commission's tenth report[10] and the voluminous correspondence of William King, bishop of Derry and archbishop of Dublin in the late seventeenth and early eighteenth century, an account of which appeared in the second report.[11]

The most complete overview of Irish archival repositories is the *Directory of Irish Archives* which includes brief descriptions of the contents of most Irish repositories, and is a useful introduction to lesser known collections which may contain Church of Ireland material. For example, the entry for the High School, Dublin reveals that it holds the records of the Erasmus Smith educational foundation which had protestant schools and estates in Counties Clare, Dublin, Galway, Tipperary, Limerick, Sligo and Waterford from the seventeenth to the twentieth century.[12] Another useful directory, although more specific in its content, is the *Directory of historic Dublin guilds*[13] which includes information on sources for trades guilds and religious confraternaties in the capital. The trade guilds controlled local government in Dublin until 1841, and, from the Reformation until the Roman Catholic relief acts of the late eighteenth century, were dominated by members of the established Church. Similar guilds operated in other Irish towns and cities, and their records are invaluable sources for the study of the Church of Ireland in early modern Ireland, for the organization of trade, and for the development of municipal corporations.[14] Religious confraternities were important social and religious foci in late medieval and early modern Ireland. They provided a medium for lay people of modest means to join together to finance the practice of obituarial prayer whereby priests were employed to say mass for the repose of the souls of former members of the confraternity. This activity was generally sited in guild chapels in parish churches and cathedrals. Following the Reformation, which largely ended this obituarial practice, these buildings passed into the custody of the Church of Ireland and much of the physical and documentary evidence of the life of the religious guilds was absorbed into the established Church. The work of Colm Lennon[15], in particular, has indicated the importance of the role of the religious confraternities in the social and religious life of Dublin. As in the case of the trades guilds, confraternities existed in other Irish towns and cities although they are less well documented.

A number of Irish repositories have published general catalogues of their manuscript holdings and some of these contain valuable details of Church of Ireland records. The Library of Trinity College, Dublin is a particularly rich source for the College was founded in the late sixteenth century to train Church of Ireland clergy and until relatively recently had a pronounced Church of Ireland ethos. Abbott's *Catalogue of manuscripts*[16] includes brief descriptions of many collections which bear upon the Church of Ireland. There are papers of prominent prelates such as James Ussher, archbishop of Armagh, 1625–56, Jonathan Swift, the eighteenth-century dean of St Patrick's cathedral, Dublin, and Joseph Stock, bishop of Killala during the 1798 Rebellion, and administrative records like the fifteenth-century register of the court of the archbishop of Dublin containing details of wills, visitations and legal processes. As well there are transcriptions of now destroyed archives such as the royal visitations of the dioceses of the Church of Ireland in the years 1615 and 1633 to 1634, which were copied by William Reeves, bishop of Down and Connor, whose archival and historical skills were so highly regarded that he was offered the post of Deputy Keeper of the public records in both Ireland and Scotland. Mark Colker's catalogue of Latin and Renaissance manuscripts in Trinity[17] provides fuller descriptions of many of the items which are summarily noted in Abbott's catalogue including ecclesiastical manuscripts which have associations with the Church of Ireland. For example, his descriptions of the book of obits of Christ Church cathedral, Dublin and the antiphonary (book of verses sung by a choir) of St John's church, Dublin are valuable for the interpretation of the membership and the liturgical practices of these late medieval urban religious communities. His identification of the ownership of individual manuscripts often provides interesting sidelights on learning in the modern Church of Ireland – why did Thomas Rundle, the eighteenth-century bishop of Derry, have a manuscript of the works of Plato, and what propelled Henry Jones, bishop of Meath, 1661–82, to remove the Book of Kells from the local parish church and present it to Trinity College?

To a lesser extent, categories of material similar to those in Trinity appear in the catalogue of manuscripts of the Gilbert Library in Dublin[18]: correspondence of bishops such as Thomas Otway, bishop of Ossory in the late seventeenth century, and William Nicholson, bishop of Derry, 1718–27; drawings and engravings of monuments in Dublin churches; and, perhaps more surprisingly, correspondence of the Cork antiquarian, Richard Caulfield (1823–87), much of it with Church of Ireland clergy who had an historical bent, relating to archaeological and historical matters in the south-west of Ireland in general and County Cork in particular in the middle years of the nineteenth century. More recently published is a *Guide to the archives of the*

Office of Public Works[19]. This is a useful introduction for those who are interested in church properties which had belonged to the established Church of Ireland but which subsequently became the property of the state: major ecclesiastical settlements such as Clonmacnoise, Glendalough and the Rock of Cashel and less well-known church sites like Ardmore, County Waterford and Kilcullen, County Kildare.

There is, regretably, no comprehensive modern guide to the holdings of the National Archives.[20] Herbert Wood's guide to the Public Record Office of Ireland is largely a catalogue of the records which were destroyed in the fire in the Four Courts in 1922 and although the post-1922 situation is interpreted to some extent by Margaret Griffith's subsequent short guide[21] this is a very brief introduction to the principal record office of the Irish state. However, the sections on parochial records and, in particular, that on non-official material are useful. The former lists those parishes for which copies of registers, in whole or in part survive, while the latter provides references to a number of useful local collections such as the records of the civil administration of the parish of St Thomas, Dublin which encompassed Luke Gardiner's fashionable eighteenth-century development of Rutland Square and Sackville Mall, Bishop Edward Synge's survey of the diocese of Elphin in 1749, and the Revd William Henry's description of Counties Sligo, Donegal and Fermanagh in 1739. In addition to the short guide, the 55th to the 59th *Report of the Deputy Keeper of the Public Records in Ireland* include summaries of accessions from 1922 to 1961 while *Sources for local studies in the Public Record Office of Ireland*[22] has useful sections on parish registers and tithe applotment books. As in Dublin, so too in Belfast there is no comprehensive guide or catalogue to the holdings of the Public Record Office of Northern Ireland which would allow researchers to identify at a distance the various categories of Church of Ireland records which are held there. However, the Belfast Record Office has conscientiously published its Deputy Keeper's reports from 1921 to 1989 and an annual report from 1990, all of which give useful information on accessions. In addition, its *Guide to church records*[23] includes listings of all Church of Ireland parish records, in original or copy form, which are available there.

Like the National Archives and the Public Record Office of Northern Ireland, the Representative Church Body Library, which is the Church of Ireland's principal repository for its archives and manuscripts, does not have a modern printed catalogue. J.B. Leslie's *Catalogue of manuscripts*[24] was published in 1938, before the Library as an archival repository had been established, and although it lists, in brief, material which is still in the collection of the Representative Church Body Library it also includes references to archives and manuscripts which are no longer present. It is, in short, seriously out of date and therefore more likely to confuse than enlighten researchers. However, although Leslie's *Catalogue* has not yet been replaced there have been a number of more recent descriptive articles on the Library's holdings. Geraldine Fitzgerald's article in *Analecta Hibernica* on 'Manuscripts in the Representative Church Body Library'[25] was followed in the 1980s and 1990s by a series of articles in genealogical, archival and historical journals: lists and indexes of the Swanzy pedigree notebooks, which relate largely to families in north-east Ulster, the pedigrees, wills and miscellaneous gleanings of the the Cork genealogist, W.H. Welply, and T.U. Sadlier's copies of marriages licences from the dioceses of Ossory[26]; descriptions of collections such as the diocesan records of Cloyne[27] and the muniments of Christ Church cathedral, Dublin[28]; and general overviews of the collection like those which appeared in *Irish Archives Bulletin, Saothar,* and *Archivium Hibernicum.*[29] In addition handlists of holdings of parish registers and vestry minute books, arranged on a county basis, are regularly produced by the Library and annual accessions lists have been printed in the *Journal of the General Synod* since 1928.

Some of the other Church of Ireland repositories (diocesan, cathedral and 'public' libraries) have from time to time published brief catalogues of their contents, and whilst most of these are now rather dated, yet, in the absence of more modern listings, they can still prove useful.[30] The most substantial of these is Newport White's catalogue of the manuscripts in Marsh's Library, Dublin[31] which includes materials from the libraries of Archbishop Narcissus Marsh, John Sterne, bishop of Clogher, and the jurist, Dudley Loftus. The collection is very miscellaneous but contains many items which might illuminate local studies: for example, memorials and letters relating to a dispute in 1781 between the Bishop of Down and Connor, Edward Smith, and James Bell, a dissenter who refused to act as a churchwarden, and an early eighteenth-century commission to value the improvements made by Alexander Cairncross, bishop of Raphoe, to his see in County Donegal. Marsh's Library was incorporated in 1707 as the first public library in Ireland and later in the century, in 1773, a similar library was established in Armagh by the then Archbishop of Armagh, Richard Robinson. This library also has a manuscript collection of which there is a brief printed catalogue.[32] Inevitably it contains much about Armagh (the cathedral, city and diocese), about the diocese of Clogher which was united to Armagh from 1850 to 1856, and about the administration of the diocese of Meath, which was the senior bishopric in the province of Armagh, particularly during the episcopate of Anthony Dopping in the late seventeenth century. Less predictable is the presence in this collection of the minute books of a Dublin club of the Apprentice Boys of Derry from 1813 to 1911. The united diocese of Down, Dromore and Connor established a library in Belfast in 1854 and by 1899 it was of sufficent significance to have a printed catalogue which included descriptions of that part of the manuscripts of William Reeves, bishop of Down and Connor, purchased by the dioceses after the bishop's death.[33] These manuscripts, which are mostly copies in whole or in part by Reeves, relate largely to ecclesiastical affairs in counties Antrim and Down (papal taxations, visitations, details of clergy, illustrations of churches) and they complement the other parts of Reeves's archive in the Royal Irish Academy, Trinity College, Dublin, and the Armagh Public Library. R.G.S. King, dean of Derry, produced a short title catalogue of the Derry Cathedral Library which includes brief accounts of two useful local collections. The Munn collection consists of thirty-two volumes of transcripts of records in British and Irish repositories relating to the city and county of Derry while the papers of the noted record agent, Tension Groves, include material about the city of Derry which was gleaned, in part, from sources in the Public Record Office of Ireland before the fire of 1922.[34]

A catalogue of the Cashel Diocesan Library was published in 1973[35] and to it was appended brief descriptions of the Library's small manuscript collection. However, apart from the early catalogues of the Library, which was amassed by Theophilus Bolton, archbishop of Cashel from 1730 to 1744, and a catalogue of the library of William King, archbishop of Dublin, which formed the core of Bolton's collection, there is little of direct Church of Ireland interest among the manuscripts. There is no catalogue of the Ross Cathedral Library in Rosscarbery, County Cork and in any case the collection has been largely dispersed. However, the brief description of it in Maura Tallon's study of Church of Ireland diocesan libraries, although largely obsolete, is in one respect still useful for she provides a description of the only manuscript in the collection: the late eighteenth-century survey by Thomas Sherrard of the estates in County Cork of Sir John Freke, which shows portions of many of the parishes in the dioceses of Cork and Ross.

Somewhat different in character to these library catalogues is Hector Love's catalogue of the records of the archbishop of Armagh[36] which lists briefly, in index form, the contents of the diocesan registry in Vicar's Hill, Armagh. The catalogue is, given its format, inevitably of limited use and has been superceded by Anthony Malcomson's comprehensive catalogue which was compiled in the late 1970s after the collection was deposited in the Public Record Office of Northern Ireland. However, its real value lies in the simple fact of its being widely available in published form whereas Dr Malcomson's work remains only as a reference tool in the Public Record Office. No other diocese has published a catalogue of its archives but there are a number of printed lists and catalogues of some of the testamentary and matrimonial collections which were in the diocesan registeries. The index to the Dublin grant books (which included wills, administrations and marriage licences) from the early seventeenth century to 1858 appeared in 1895[37] and was quickly followed by Sir Arthur Vicars's index to the prerogative wills of Ireland, 1536–1810[38], H.F. Berry's edition of the register of wills and inventories of the diocese of Dublin for the years 1457–1483[39] and indexes to the marriage licence bonds of Cork, Cloyne and Ross for the seventeenth and eighteenth centuries[40]. Between 1909 and 1920 five volumes of indexes to Irish wills were published by Phillimore[41] and in 1930 Fr Wallace Clare's *Guide to copies and abstracts of Irish wills* appeared[42]. More recently indexes to wills, administrations and marriage licence bonds have been published in the *The Irish Ancestor*.[43]

However, if there are few catalogues of Irish ecclesiastical records and even fewer exclusively devoted to the archives of the Church or Ireland, there are a number of general source books which discuss Church of Ireland records. Among the best of these are *Irish church records*[44], *Sources for early modern Irish history*[45], *Irish towns: a guide to sources*[46] and *Tracing the past*[47] which have valuable chapters on ecclesiastical records while *Sources of Irish local history*[48], although a little dated, is still useful. *Irish records*[49] and *Tracing your Irish ancestors*[50], although written chiefly from a genealogical perspective, are also helpful, particularly the former which includes sketch maps of the parishes in each county. Similar maps are printed in *A new genealogical atlas of Ireland*.[51] *British sources for Irish history, 1485–1641*[52] contains some nuggets of Church of Ireland material in local repositories in Great Britain, such as a list of entries from the Court of Faculties muniment books in Lambeth Palace Library, London which includes information on clergy in Meath, Kildare, Down, Dublin and Wexford, and *Papers of British churchmen, 1780–1940*[53] has brief descriptions of the collections of Church of Ireland bishops and clergy in repositories in Great Britain and Ireland.

While published histories, catalogues and guides can provide an important introduction to local research they are, in most instances, only part of the preparation for the real work which will require the use of original source material with all the challenges of access and interpretation that such endeavour involves. However, a useful bridge between printed and manuscript material is the not inconsiderable body of published editions, both complete text editions and detailed calendars, of archives and manuscripts which is available. Such works have a number of obvious advantages. First they are published and therefore available in research libraries, although in the case of older editions which may have been produced in limited numbers, they may not be as generally accessible as might be wished. Secondly, they are printed and therefore easier to read than the original documents, and, in the case of manuscripts which have been written in a language other than English, they may also provide a translation. Thirdly, they invariably include an introduction, usually by an expert in the field, which provides intellectual access to what otherwise may appear to be an obscure text, and an index which allows a more selective use of the source than would otherwise be possible.

The written legacy of the early Church is relatively well served by printed editions of texts of annals, lives of the saints and liturgical works many of which are closely associated with particular localities. Individual editions of the most famous of the insular manuscripts, the Book of Kells[54], Book of Durrow[55] and Book of Armagh[56], are readily available while other less famous but equally important liturgical texts, such as the Antiphonary of Bangor, County Down[57] and the Martyrology of Tallaght[58] have been published by the Henry Bradshaw Society or, like the Kilcormac missal from County Offaly, printed as part of the transactions of the Royal Irish Academy[59]. Charles Plummer's *Lives of the Irish saints*[60] is an invaluable introduction to Irish hagiography with the added bonus of texts in both Irish and English, while Gearóid MacNiochaill's booklet on medieval annals provides a valuable critique of the topic and a useful bibliography of manuscript and printed sources.[61]

Happily a good many of the, admittedly few, extant medieval Irish church archives have been printed. There are editions of five of the seven medieval registers of the archbishops of Armagh[62], of the two surviving Dublin diocesan registers[63] and of the Red Book of Ossory[64] and the Black Book of Limerick.[65] The Black and White Books of Christ Church Cathedral, Dublin, have been calendared[66] and there are editions of the book of obits and martyology[67] and of the fourteenth-century account rolls[68], while for St Patrick's cathedral, Dublin, editions of the Dignitas Decani[69] and the Dublin Troper[70] have also been published. The records of other monastic houses, apart from Christ Church cathedral, are also printed. Substantial Dublin foundations such as St Mary's Abbey[71], the Priory of All Hallows[72] and the Abbey of St Thomas[73] were obviously attractive to editors but registers of rural houses such as the priory at Tristernagh, near Kilbixy, County Westmeath[74] were also printed as were cartularies (monastic registers) from British houses with Irish associations like the Augustinian foundation of Llanthony[75] which had houses in Monmouthshire, Gloucestershire and County Meath. Shorter pieces, such as the fifteenth and sixteenth-century episcopal rentals of Clonfert and Kilmacduagh and have appeared from time to time in *Annalecta Hibernica*[76].

Church archives from the modern period have also been printed but in proportion to the quantity of material available the output has been much less than for the medieval period. The Parish Register Society of Dublin published, between 1906 and 1915, twelve volumes of registers of baptisms, marriages and burials[77], and in recent years the Representative Church Body Library has revived this project[78]. Editions of diocesan records such as the late seventeenth-century court book of St Sepulchre's, which was a liberty within the jurisdiction of the archbishop of Dublin[79], and Bishop Dive Downes's visitation of the dioceses of Cork and Ross in 1699[80] have been valuable for local studies and Raymond Gillespie's work on the early modern muniments of Christ Church cathedral, Dublin has done much to revive interest in cathedral communities[81]. Many smaller documents have been printed in the journals of local history societies and in the publications of national and provincial learned bodies. For example the early nineteenth-century visitation records of Charles Lindsay, bishop of Kildare, appeared in the Kildare Archaeological Society's journal[82] while Archbishop Bulkley's visitation of Dublin in 1630 was printed in *Archivium Hibernicum*, the journal of the Catholic Record Society of Ireland[83]. R.J. Hayes's compendious listing of articles in Irish periodicals[84] is an invaluable guide to such material.

Those primary sources which might not, in the most obvious sense of the word, be construed as archives – gravestones and memorials, church plate, and portraits – are also to varying extents accessible through the medium of published lists and indexes. The Association for the Preservation of the Memorials of the Dead, Ireland published an annual journal from 1888 to 1937 which included, in a rather chaotic fashion, inscriptions from many Church of Ireland graveyards and, more recently, the Ulster Historical Foundation has sponsored a *Gravestone Inscriptions* series which has catalogued many Church of Ireland graveyards in Counties Antrim and Down[85]. Much additional transcription has been done by, for example, Brian Cantwell in counties Wicklow and Wexford and Michael Egan in Dublin[86], and many enthusiastic amateurs continue this good work throughout the country and publish their transcriptions in local history and genealogical journals. A number of catalogues of church plate have been published, notably Webster's illustrated catalogue of the plate of the dioceses of Cork, Cloyne and Ross[87], Seymour's list of the plate of Cashel and Emly[88], and Tony Sweeny's illustrated catalogue of Irish Stuart silver[89] which includes references to many Church of Ireland pieces, while an impression of the Church's collection of portraits may be had from a list which was published in 1916[90]. A useful general introduction to Church of Ireland plate, portraits and topographical prints and drawings is the catalogue of an exhibition which was held in the National Gallery of Ireland to mark the centenary of the disestablishment of the Church of Ireland.[91]

II. PHYSICAL ACCESS: VISITING THE LIBRARIES AND ARCHIVES

When the histories have been scanned, the catalogues consulted, and the printed editions and their introductions ruthlessly pillaged the time will be ripe for researchers to visit the repositories and other locations in which the archives and the manuscripts of the Church of Ireland are to be found. Such visits will allow researchers to follow up the leads which they have obtained from the introductory printed material but, more importantly, will introduce them to the great majority of Church of Ireland records which have not been edited for publication and which do not appear in printed catalogues.

Church of Ireland archives and manuscripts are to be found in two custodies – repositories, usually archives and libraries, both publicly and privately funded, and 'local custody', that is, with the clergy, church officers, parishes, dioceses, cathedrals and organizations that created the records. These two custodies present different challenges to the researcher and within both categories there will be varients of practice which may in turn delight and exasperate.

The collections in publicly funded repositories, in theory at least, are the most accessible and those in the National Archives, National Library, Public

Record Office of Northern Ireland, Trinity College, Dublin and the Royal
Irish Academy, in particular, cannot be ignored by any serious local historian
who is interested in Church of Ireland archives and manuscripts. Although all
these repositories depend upon government funding for their existence their
attitude to members of the public varies and the eager reader is not always
given the impression of a right of public access to the collections. Formalities
vary but may include the need to make an appointment, an interview and the
issue of a reader's ticket for which a letter of introduction and a photograph
may be necessary and for which a fee may be charged. Having been granted
admission, readers will have to master the repository's finding aids which are
the essential means of local intellectual access to the great mass of archives and
manuscripts which have not been described in printed catalogues. This tends
to be somewhat more daunting in the large public repositories since their
collections are very various and the Church of Ireland dimension within them
is rarely a priority for the curatorial staff. In most institutions a card catalogue,
either a single integrated catalogue or one which is divided thematically
(places, persons, subjects etc), will provide initial access and references from
the catalogue to summary typescript catalogues or detailed handlists of
particular collections will allow the researcher to establish more clearly the
potential value of the material for their research. For the diligent researcher,
who is prepared to spend time with each repository's finding aids, there are
great riches to be uncovered.

The National Archives, as the principal archival repository of the Irish
state, remains a useful source for Church of Ireland material for despite the
enormous losses in 1922 much relevant material has been subsequently
accessioned and invaluable copy and extract material, which makes good some
of the losses has been obtained. The original records of a number of parishes,
the tithe applotment books for parishes in the Republic of Ireland, the
surviving records of the Ecclesiastical Commissioners and the Irish Church
Temporalities Commissioners, and the indexes to matrimonial and testamentary
records are complemented by, for example, the growing collection of copy
wills, a body of miscellaneous extracts and certified copies from parish registers,
and copies of various diocesan and cathedral records. However, perhaps the
single most significant Church of Ireland collection in the National Archives
is the archive of the central administration of the Protestant Orphan Society[92]
which complements the records of the various county orphan societies. A
general card catalogue introduces readers to the collections for some of which
there are more detailed handlists.

In the National Library, the Department of Manuscripts has the most
comprehensive collection of Irish family papers and inevitably these include
many little known collections which illuminate local life from a Church of
Ireland perspective. The papers of Robert Howard, successively bishop of
Killala and Elphin in the first half of the eighteenth century[93], are, as the work

of Toby Barnard has revealed, an invaluable source for learning and literacy in the west of Ireland[94] while the collections of Church of Ireland families such as Smyth of Barbavilla, County Westmeath[95], or converts to anglicanism like French of Monivea, County Galway[96], can document in extraordinary detail the lives of many who lived in the localities in which such families held sway. Hayes's *Manuscript sources* provides a short title catalogue of the National Library collections up to 1975 and a card catalogue provides access to more recent accessions.

For those whose research is based on places or people in Northern Ireland, or to a lesser extent in the other three counties of the historic province of Ulster, a visit to the Public Record Office in Belfast is essential. The Record Office website provides a general introduction to the Office[97] while databases of prominent persons, places and subjects, a card index of personal names, and colour coded handlists (black for church records and green for microfilm copies) in the search room can quickly guide researchers to relevent material. In archival terms the Record Office in Belfast is, in effect, the Church of Ireland repository for Northern Ireland (rather in the same way in which each diocese of the Church of England usually nominates one of the county record offices as the diocesan record centre) and holds considerable collections of parish and diocesan records as well as the tithe applotment books for parishes in Northern Ireland. All Church of Ireland parish registers, in copy or original form, are available there and an increasing number of parishes are depositing other categories of records – vestry minute books, accounts, preachers' books etc. Records from the dioceses of Armagh, Clogher, Derry, Down and Dromore, and Connor have been transferred to Belfast. In addition, like the Representative Church Body Library in Dublin, the Record Office holds collections of papers of significant church figures such as Lord John George Beresford, archbishop of Armagh, 1822–62,[98] and the antiquarian cleric, W.A. Reynell, who copied much valuable material from the Board of First Fruits office[99], as well as records of local organizations like the Protestant Orphan Society[100] or the Belfast Church Extension Society which charts the development of the Church of Ireland in the developing suburbs of the city in the late nineteenth and early twentieth century[101]. Also included in the collections are papers of the great anglican titled families like the Abercorns, Downshires and Dunleaths who contributed much to the Church especially in rural Ulster[102]; and a bewildering array of civil archives, photographs and miscellaneous papers which can illuminate innumerable aspects of the life of the Church of Ireland in many localities.

The same is true of the Manuscripts Room in the Library of Trinity College, Dublin whose printed catalogues cover only a fraction of the Church of Ireland material which is available. Most importantly, there is no published guide to the large collection of College records which bear on the Church of Ireland in many ways. The College, as we have seen, was founded in the late sixteenth century, essentially as a Church of Ireland seminary, and until this century the vast majority of its students were Church of Ireland. Moreover, until 1873 its fellows had to be Church of Ireland clergy although there were dispensations from this obligation. Until 1980 Church of Ireland clergy were trained in the college's divinity school, and until 1973 the services in the college chapel were exclusively Church of Ireland. Therefore, the documentation which the administration of the College produced inevitably is an important source for the Church of Ireland, not only in Dublin and not only in the area of university education, but also throughout Ireland for clergy who were trained in Trinity served in parishes throughout the country and brought their own particular flavour to local life. Furthermore the College owned extensive landed estates in Ulster and Munster and the associated advowsons of a number of parishes. These positions were largely reserved for fellows of the College who wished to return to parish life, and so a significant number of parishes enjoyed clergy of unusual intellectual emminence and occassional eccentricity. The historian, Thomas Leland, resigned his fellowship in 1781 to become rector of Newtownstewart in the wilds of County Tyrone while in 1822 the astronomer and mathematician, Thomas Romney Robinson, later to become president of the Royal Irish Academy, resigned to become rector of Enniskillen.[103] Much information on the background of the local clergy and the careers of the fellows may be obtained from the college muniments.

As in the case of the muniments, many of the manuscript collections are not detailed in published catalogues. Abbott's *Catalogue* appeared in 1900 and there has been no general catalogue published since then. However, a card catalogue, cumulative index and detailed handlists will guide readers through the considerable accessions since *Abbott* and will help to identify sources for the study of the Church of Ireland. The Trinity collection includes episcopal correspondence such as that of the nineteenth-century bishop of Limerick, John Jebb[104], or William Bennet[105], who became bishop of Cork in 1790; diaries like those of the Revd Daniel Beaufort detailing his travels in Ireland in the early nineteenth century[106]; letters of local clergy such as the Revd Charles Claudius Beresford who was rector of Bailieborough in County Cavan during the Great Famine[107]. In addition there are copies of, now lost, church records such as those made by William Reeves, bishop of Down and Connor, largely from sources in the Public Record Office of Ireland[108] and those of the Cork antiquary, Richard Caulfield, from the Cork diocesan archives[109]. Furthermore the records of organizations with close associations with the Church of Ireland such as the Irish Society[110], the Island and Coast Society[111] and the Hibernian Marine Society[112] contain valuable information on those who were involved in missionary and educational work on the geographical peripheries of Ireland.

In the Royal Irish Academy a card catalogue and a two-volume typescript list, prepared by Patrick Cosgrave in 1965, supplement Hayes's *Manuscript sources* in guiding researchers through the manuscript collections. The papers of William Reeves, bishop of Down and Connor, the Revd James Graves, the renowned Irish antiquarian, and H.R. Dawson, dean of St Patrick's cathedral, Dublin, 1828–40, who corresponded on historical and antiquarian subjects with among others, Richard Butler, vicar of Trim, James Saurin, archdeacon of Dromore, and George Dwyer, rector of Ardrahan, County Galway[113], are all of potential local interest. So too are stray Church of Ireland archives such as visitations of the diocese of Ossory in 1845 and 1848[114], and copies of now lost records such as appear in James Ferguson's précises of documents (leases, grants, letters) relating to parishes in the dioceses of Dublin and Glendalough from the fourteenth to the nineteenth century[115], and copies of records (rentals, tithe records, visitations) of the dioceses of Down and Connor in the seventeenth and eighteenth century[116]. Perhaps the richest source for local studies among the Academy's manuscript collections and one which contains much about the Church of Ireland is the Ordnance Survey memoirs and related papers. These contain detailed accounts of many of the parishes of Ireland in the mid-nineteenth century and inevitably include much valuable information about buildings which had been or continued to be used as Church of Ireland churches and cathedrals. The forty published volumes of memoirs[117] cover the counties of Antrim, Armagh, Donegal, Down, Fermanagh, Londonderry and Tyrone with some additional material for counties Cavan, Leitrim, Louth, Monaghan and Sligo. The complementary thirty five volumes of unpublished letters contain ' . . . information relative to the antiquities . . .' of virtually every parish in the country.

The Representative Church Body Library in Dublin is the Church of Ireland's principal repository for its archives and manuscripts and all researchers are welcome to use its facilities. Personal interrogation is kept to a minimum, there are no readers' tickets issued, no entrance fees charged and no appointments required: basic information on how to get there and what to expect is available on the Church of Ireland website[118]. Essentially the Library holds those non-current records of the Church of Ireland in the Republic of Ireland which the parishes, dioceses, cathedrals and central administration have chosen to transfer to it. There is as yet no requirement to tranfer non-current records to the Library and the extent to which transfers have occurred varies throughout the country. There is therefore nothing inevitable about the Library's archival holdings and some materials which researchers might reasonably expect to have been transferred may still be in 'local custody'. The Library's holdings are further defined by legislation: older parish registers[119] are public records in Northern Ireland and national archives in the Republic and may not be moved from one political jurisdiction to the other. In order to avoid splitting collections the Church of Ireland has agreed a policy with the Public Record Office in Belfast that all non-current records in Northern Ireland will be transferred to Belfast rather than to the Library in Dublin.

However, since dioceses and even parishes straddle the border there are occasional exceptions to this policy.

At present the Library holds records from over 660 parishes, seventeen dioceses, and fifteen cathedrals, mostly in the Republic of Ireland; the minutes, reports and related documentation of the General Synod, Representative Church Body, and their statutory committees, since disestablishment; and the records of a variety of fixed term committees and commissions which have been set up to examine particular aspects of the Church's life. Access to most of this material is straightforward. The *Constitution of the Church of Ireland* explicitly recognises a right of public access to all parish registers of baptisms, marriages and burials and so there are no restrictions on making these records available. Otherwise, the Library operates in accordance with normal archival procedures: there is a thirty year rule (that is, records which are less than thirty years old are not usually made available to researchers) and material which is deemed to be of a sensitive nature may be closed for longer periods. In the particular case of the manuscript records of the General Synod and Representative Church Body, the permission of the appropriate administrative officer in Church of Ireland House is required before the Library can produce these records for researchers. However, the vast majority of Church of Ireland archives are available for consulation without restriction. A general card catalogue will guide researchers to people, places and a variety of subjects which occur in the collections and these topics may be explored in more detail in the series of handlists of parish, diocesan and cathedral records.

One class of record in the Library which sits a little apart from the official archives of the Church is the large body of architectural drawings which may be a stray remnant of the archive of the Ecclesiastical Commissioners. The component parts of this collection are a six-volume survey of churches in the province of Cashel by James Pain, dating probably from the second quarter of the nineteenth century[120]; four mid-nineteenth century volumes of drawings of churches largely, but not exclusively, in the province of Tuam, and mostly by Joseph Welland[121]; and twenty-seven portfolios of drawings of churches from all parts of Ireland, and by various architects, dating from the 1830s to the 1860s, with more recent accessions.[122] Both Pain and Welland were distinguished architects having worked for the Board of First Fruits and the Ecclesiastical Commissioners as were figures such as William Atkins, Frederick Darley, and the partnership of Lanyon and Lynn, whose work is also represented in the collection.

In addition to the official archives of the Church of Ireland the Library also holds over 630 collections of miscellaneous manuscripts consisting for the most part of papers of clergy and laity and records of voluntary organizations which are closely related to the Church of Ireland. As well the Library is developing an oral history archive, a photograph collection, and a database of information on church plate, and holds a growing body of information on the Church of Ireland portrait collection.

In recent years the Library has become a focus for the papers of bishops, clergy and laity. Episcopal collections such as the correspondence of Euseby Cleaver who was bishop of Ferns at the time of the 1798 rebellion[123] and Lord John Beresford who was archbishop of Armagh at the height of the tithe war[124], can provide valuable local insights into national events. The diaries of the Revd Stephen Gwynn are a useful window into north Antrim life in the second half of the nineteenth century[125] while the daily weather notes of Henry Cotton, archdeacon of Cashel, for the 1820s and 1830s provide a period insight into a perennial topic of Irish conversation[126] and the papers of Hugh Maude, a prominent County Dublin layman, reveal much about the Church of Ireland's response to constitutional, liturgical and administrative change in the 1940s and 1950s[127]. The research papers of clergy who had used local and national collections in the late nineteenth and early twentieth centuries have, since the destruction of 1922, assumed an enhanced significance and there are useful examples of such collections in the Library apart from the papers of Leslie and his colleagues who worked on clerical successions. The notes of the Revd James Graves relating to the medieval diocese of Ossory which were taken from the Irish memoranda and plea rolls[128] and the Revd W.H. Rennison's unpublished research into the history of the diocese of Waterford[129] are examples of this genre.

Equally rich as sources for the Church of Ireland in the localities are the records of a wide range of organizations and societies, mostly with their origins in the nineteenth century, which touched the faithful and those who were distressed in body, mind or estate. The records of the nineteenth and twentieth-century clerical societies provide an entrée into the social, spiritual and educational world of local rectors, while organizations such as the Nenagh Young Men's Christian and Literary Association, founded in 1861 for the moral, educational and social advancement of the young men of the town[130], or the City of Dublin Conservative Working Men's Club[131], are interesting sources for the history of local recreation. The poor and disadvantaged are catalogued in the records of bodies such as the Protestant Orphan Society which was organized on a county basis[132] or the Association for the Relief of Distressed Protestants[133], while the rescue of 'fallen women' is chronicled in the records of the Prison Gate Mission[134] and the Magdalen Asylum, Dublin[135]. The Church, too, was closely involved in the education of children and the training of teachers. The records of organizations such as the Incorporated Society for Promoting Protestant Schools in Ireland, which had a presence in virtually every county in Ireland[136], and the Church Education Society[137] reveal this in a national context and the records of schools like the Irish Clergy Daughters' School[138], Dublin, Bishop Foy's School, Waterford[139] and Bishop Hodson's Grammar School, Elphin[140] provide evidence of such activity in the localities.

The archives of the Church and the records of organizations and individuals for the more recent past are complemented by the oral recollections and reminicences of clergy and laity. The development of this oral archive is in its infancy and most of the initial tranche of recordings will be closed to readers during the lifetime of the interviewees but the determination of the Church of Ireland to record the experiences not only of the leaders of the Church but also of the men and women in the pews suggests that in time this may be an invaluable supplement to the official record. Since the experiences of the majority of church people are confined to a small number of localities this promises to be an important source for local studies. It also emphasises the importance, for those whose research in centred on the recent past, of seeking out the experiences of older members of the community. Like the oral history project, the photographic archive is a relatively recent innovation and still very much 'work in progress'. The majority of photographs which have been collected and commissioned are of church buildings but there is a growing body of visual information on clergy, laity, events and artifacts, including church plate.

Conditions of access to the manuscripts collection are similar to those which relate to Church of Ireland archives. A thirty year rule is in operation and some collections or parts of collections are closed for longer periods. The general card catalogue provides immediate access to the collections, a summary catalogue offers short descriptions of each collection, and detailed handlists are available for most of, although not all, the material. Access to the photograph collection is more limited although the combination of the general card catalogue and a handlist will usually satisfy the needs of researchers. There is no direct reader access, for reasons of sensitivity and security, to the oral archive, church plate database or to the inventories of portraits but the Library staff will evaluate the validity of requests for information from these sources and where appropriate respond positively.

Access to some of the other Church of Ireland repositories is less certain although there is invariably a willingness to be accommodating. The two 'public libraries', Archbishop Marsh's Library in Dublin and Archbishop Robinson's Library in Armagh are the most accessible with regular staff and public opening hours, and, in the case of Marsh's an introduction on the internet.[141] Admittance to the collections in the libraries in Cashel, Derry and Ross is dependent to a large extent on the deans of these cathedrals. It would, therefore, be prudent for researchers to write in advance establishing their *bona fides* and stating clearly the material which they wish to see, and to follow up their letter with a telephone call to ensure that before they travel all is well.

In terms of access to Church of Ireland records, the greatest difficulties occur with material which is in 'local custody'. There is as yet no requirement to transfer non-current Church of Ireland archives to the Representative Church Body Library or to the Record Office in Belfast. Most of the archives of the central administration in Dublin, and of the dioceses and cathedrals have been transferred as have a substantial number of parish collections. However, a significant quantity of parish records remains in local churches, rectories and parish offices and access to them is through the medium of the local clergy whose addresses and telephone numbers are usually the only readily available points of contact. The clergy are required by the *Constitution of the Church of Ireland* to ' . . . at all reasonable times, on demand, allow search in such registers [of baptisms, marriages and burials] . . . ' and whilst there is a general willingness to accommodate researchers in the spirit of this obligation nevertheless there are frequently practical problems in fullfilling it. Most obviously, problems arise because most Church of Ireland clergy work alone: few have curates and even fewer are part of a team ministry in which administrative responsibility can be shared among members of a group of clergy and laity. Some urban parishes will have an office in which researchers can consult parish records in a comfortable and supervised environment without the attendance of the local clergy but this is the exception to the rule. In most instances 'local access' means that the local clergy must produce the records and personally supervise the search in a church vestry which will usually be a cold and unattractive location, or in the rectory, which is the clergy residence and in which researchers may, in effect, be intruding on family life. In consequence a lone cleric may, at times, be unable to accommodate researchers with the expedition that they consider to be appropriate. Students invariably believe that their work is a priority and whilst it ought to be so for them it cannot always be so for local clergy who may have to conduct marriages, visit the sick and dying and bury the dead, among a host of other parochial duties, as well as considering the needs of their families.

Despite these potential difficulties it is important to stress that there is, in most instances, a ready willingnesss among local clergy to help, but researchers will greatly help themselves and increase the liklihood of ready access to the collections in which they are interested by taking some basic preparatory steps. They need first to establish not only that the records survive for a particular locality but that they are extant for the appropriate period, and then they must discover who has custody of these records. Inventories of most parish records are held in the Representative Church Body Library and it is usually possible to advise researchers, with a fair degree of accuracy, if the records which they are seeking are extant. The names and addresses of the clergy and the churches for which they are responsible are published annually in the *Church of Ireland Directory* which is available in printed form in most reference libraries or, in a limited form, on the Church of Ireland website[142]. However, the *Directory* has three limitations. First, it concentrates on churches which are still open for worship and some local research will require access to the records of closed churches and their parishes; secondly, there are frequent changes to the clerical directory in the course of a year and as the *Directory* is an annual publication parts of it can be out of date; and thirdly, there will from time to time be vacant parishes (that is parishes without a resident priest or deacon) and so the *Directory* will not supply a contact name, address or telephone number. For those with access to the internet the clerical directory on the Church of Ireland website is periodically updated during the year: otherwise, the easiest way of dealing with these deficiencies is to contact the Representative Church Body Library where the staff can supply information on redundant churches and details of local contacts.

Once a researcher has established that appropriate records survive and has determined who has custody of them the following procedure is recommended. Write to the local custodian, enclosing a letter of credence, setting out, as clearly as the introductory sources have permitted, which records are required; follow up the letter after a short time with a telephone call to make an appointment to see the records; and immediately before travelling telephone again to ensure that the arrangement still obtains. If such arrangements do not produce access to local records researchers should contact the Representative Church Body Library where the staff may be able to set up a local appointment or arrange to have the records transferred temporarily to the Library for research purposes. Clergy are entitled to charge a fee for supervising searches and whilst many do not ask for payment researchers should be financially prepared.

The interpretation of Church of Ireland
archives and manuscripts

Although the major challenge for those using Church of Ireland archives and manuscripts may appear to be to identify, locate and gain access to them, yet these challenges having been met, problems of interpretation may remain. In other words, it is one thing to find oneself eventually seated before the much sought after materials, but it may be a step further to make sense of their contents and to place them in an appropriate context, for there are both strengths and weaknesses about Church of Ireland records of which the student needs to be aware.

The most obvious strengths of Church of Ireland records are their chronological span and geographical scope. It is worth reiterating that the Church is the oldest extant institution in Ireland: older than the state, older than the municipalities, older than the schools and universities, older in short than all those Irish institutions which are constantly trumpeting their longevity in a seemingly endless round of anniversary celebrations. There may still be debate about when and in what circumstances Christianity was brought to this country and there may still be differences of opinion about the lines of succession from the early Church following the fracturing of Christianity in the west in the sixteenth century, nonetheless what is beyond dispute is the venerability of the shared heritage of the celtic and medieval Church in Ireland and the astonishing talent for survival which the Church of Ireland has exhibited since the Reformation. The monastic Church in Ireland, the dioceses, cathedrals and parishes, largely created by the Normans, the established Church which emerged from the Reformation, and the disestablished Church of Ireland which succeeded it in the late nineteenth century are the principal phases of a continuum of Christian worship, the written legacy of which is or has been the responsibility of the Church of Ireland. The survival of manuscript material for some parts of Ireland over such an extended period offers remarkable scope for the perceptive and persistent local historian.

Inevitably, of course, the places, families and institutions which can be studied over a protracted period are limited but what is, within the physical confines of the island of Ireland, almost unlimited are the locations in which the Church of Ireland, for good or ill, has had a presence or an effect. The establishment of the parish system and its development to meet the constantly changing needs of rural and urban life introduced the Church to old and new communities throughout the country. During the period of the established

Church, in particular, the Church of Ireland as both a religious and civil power, touched the lives of most classes of Irish men and women. The nobility and gentry who occupied grand houses in town and country, worshipped in the great cathedrals, were leading lights in the parish churches, and exercised patronage in ecclesiastical livings. The agricultural classes were tenants of bishops, cathedral chapters and parishes and supported the Church, willingly or unwillingly, with their tithes. The teeming hordes in the cities and towns in life availed of the religious and social services which the Church had to offer and in death filled the graveyards of the town and city churches.

However, wide though the chronolgical and geographical scope of Church of Ireland records can be, their usefulness is inevitably circumscribed by two key considerations: first the Church of Ireland was always a minority Church, and secondly, many of its records no longer survive. Even at the height of its powers the Church of Ireland never commanded the loyalty, nominal or otherwise, much less the affection, of the majority of the people of Ireland. Despite penal legislation and the clearly perceived social and economic advantages of membership, the church 'as by law established' had to compete with the Roman Catholic Church and the dissenting traditions for the support of the people. Many families, therefore, have no Church of Ireland tradition while for others the links with the established Church were so nominal as to be of only passing significance. An elder son may have conformed to retain his family's ownership of land only to revert to the 'one true Church' when it was safe to do so while 'notorious Methodists', as they were sometimes described in clergy visiting books, may have availed of the Church of Ireland only for the christian rites of passage but did not allow such necessities to temper their Wesleyan life style. More generally, tenants may have held land from, or may have been employed by, Church of Ireland proprietors without any more than a perfunctory nod in the direction of anglicanism. Inevitably, therefore, the records of the Church of Ireland will not tell the full story of Irish communities and, furthermore, the story which they can tell has been inhibited by the loss of so many records. Late medieval and early modern Irish society was less developed, less prosperous, less sophisticated and less stable than in England or continental Europe. It produced, relatively, fewer archives and manuscripts and did not develop or retain sufficient centres of learning which could have fostered an appreciation of the importance of such materials and which might have provided the environment in which the safe transmission of records from one generation to the next could have been ensured. There were no medieval universities in imitation of Bologna, Paris, Oxford or Cambridge and the monasteries, once dissolved, were not replaced with any significant alternative centres of learning: the Catholic clergy were trained abroad while the Church of Ireland did not establish a seminary until the foundation of Trinity College in 1592. The Viking invasions, the dissolution of the monasteries and the Reformation, the 1641 Rebellion, the

Commonwealth, the Jacobite and Williamite wars, and the 1798 Rebellion produced a litany of violence and disorder which repeatedly violated the fragile Irish ecclesiastical archival infrastructure. Even when the archives of Church and state seemed secure, with the establishment of a Public Record Office in Dublin and the transfer to it of much of the surviving national documentation, the violence of civil war, in an act of supreme irony, reduced to ashes the written evidence of the nation which the protagonists in the conflict sought so passionately to define. The destruction of many of the records of parishes, dioceses, cathedrals and of the central govenment, of which the Church of Ireland was an integral part, dealt the Church an enormous blow for despite the survival of copy material, the ingenious use of civil records, and the evidence of archaeology and architecture, parts of the history of many Church of Ireland communities cannot be adequately researched because the sources no longer exist.

But other parts of the history of the Church of Ireland cannot be researched for a different reason: because the Church will not allow it. There is a tendency, perhaps understandable in an age when freedom of information is increasingly taken to be a societal norm, to assume that there is an automatic right of access to Church of Ireland records for interested researchers: but this is not so. The Church of Ireland is a private organization and its archives, with the exception of parish registers, access to which is guaranteed under civil and ecclesiastical law, are owned totally and absolutely by the Church which is not obliged to make them available for historical research. That the Church chooses to make most of its records available to researchers may tend to obscure the basic fact that such availablity is a privilege and not a right, and there are occasions on which this privilege is not extended to researchers. This is particularly so in the context of more recent records which in the case of the Church of Ireland may involve almost any aspect of the Church's life since disestablishment. The Church of Ireland in the twentieth century, especially in the Republic of Ireland, is a small, closely knit community with a long memory, all of which makes it, at times, particularly cautious about publicly discussing aspects of its affairs which it considers to be sensitive. Thus, for example, the records of the House of Bishops, which it may be presumed has been a forum for considering many controversial issues which affected the Church on both an institutional and personal level, are not available to researchers; the minutes and related papers of the General Synod and the Representative Body may be seen only with the permission of the administration in Church of Ireland House in Dublin; while the records of many charitable bodies are closed for what may appear to readers to be unreasonably long periods but which, in the context of a small community which values the privacy of its members, seems entirely appropriate. Such limitations on research may irritate readers and there may be a temptation to seek to circumvent restrictions on collections by personal appeals to higher authorities within the Church. Such activity is invariably counterproductive for it will result in the researcher losing the goodwill of the archival community.

Yet despite destruction and restriction a sufficient corpus of material is available to allow at least a partial historical reconstruction of much of the Church's history. However, the effective use of much of this material is inhibited because it is uncatalogued, and of that which has been processed many collections would benefit from more detailed attention from archivists. This is particularly true of the larger diocesan and cathedral archives and some of the more significant collections of papers of modern churchmen which contain considerable quantities of individual documents that are very time consuming to process. These need to be sorted, arranged and listed before being made available to researchers, not only for administrative and security purposes, but also because the production of a detailed handlist, as well as providing descriptions of the individual elements of the collection, place those items in an overall context which itself can be informative for a student. Irish archival life has developed significantly in recent years but is still enormously under resourced and it is difficult to be optimistic that in the short term the considerable cataloguing backlogs, both in the Church of Ireland repositories, and in the publicly funded archives and libraries which hold significant Church of Ireland material, can be substantially reduced. Ironically the upsurge in interest in local history and the demands of researchers for information, advice and access to records are among the principal reasons for the continued problems with cataloguing: more researchers occupy more staff time and leave even less than before for cataloguing! An inevitable consequence of these problems of cataloguing has been a lack of printed guides to Church of Ireland collections in the various repositories. Such publications, by their very nature, are distillations of generations of detailed handlists but since much of that basic work for the Church of Ireland has yet to be done, the publication of guides would be premature.

This lack of handlists and guides has the unfortunate consequence of making the student too dependent on the small archival community who professionally service Church of Ireland collections. These archivists and librarians are not teachers, they may not necessarily have an historical background, they may not even be members of the Church of Ireland, and they certainly are not polymaths. Most will know a certain amount about the collections in their care but they will not have an encyclopaedic knowledge about all aspects of all collections and there is an inevitability that their advice will be coloured more by the state of their particular knowledge rather than by their possession of a comprehensive overview of Church of Ireland sources. Furthermore, in the larger national institutions, there is a tendency to move curatorial staff from department to department and whilst this ensures a greater degree of professional flexibility within an institution it also militates against archival staff remaining long enough in a post to build up a substantial body of knowledge about the collections in their care. The lack of finding aids creates problems not only for students but also for teachers, a significant number of whom seem to be unaware of the holdings of many Irish repositories. It cannot be sufficiently stressed that archivists and librarians are not directors of studies and that students who assume that they are will most likely be disappointed.

The interpretation of Church of Ireland records, in a more particular sense, may require a range of linguistic and paleographic skills which are now rarely taught. One of the less obvious strengths of post-Reformation Church of Ireland records is that they are almost invariably written in English, in contrast to Roman Catholic records for which Latin continued to be the language of record until the reforms of the second Vatican Council. However, those who intend to work on the archives of the medieval church will require a knowledge of Latin and, in some instances, of Norman French which was the administrative language of the Norman kings of England, for while many of the texts have been printed not all have been translated. A competence in school Latin, aided by a good dictionary and Baxter and Johnston's *Medieval Latin word-list*[1] will usually suffice but those with no Latin at all need to seriously consider whether the time spent in word for word translation is justifiable when so much material is available in English. Yet even those records which are written in English may present some problems for those who are not familiar with earlier forms of writing, particularly in the sixteenth and seventeenth centuries. However, the understanding of handwriting is, in most instances, a matter of familiarity and frequent exposure to manuscript texts, with the assistance, initially, of a paleographic guide[2], will satisfy the needs of most researchers. From the middle of the eighteenth century handwritten English, with the exception of the use of the long letter E (similar to a modern letter F), is sufficiently similar to modern usage so as to present no real problems for modern readers: however, archaic forms of writing continued to be used occasionally until late in the century. But if the forms of the letters are fairly obvious from the 1780s on, there remains the eternal problem of bad handwriting which can render obscure even the simplest communication. The Church of Ireland did not begin to use typewriters for its central records until the 1930s while at local level handwritten minutes were the norm until the 1960s and handwriting continues to be the form in which parish registers are maintained.

Those who find difficulty with handwriting may be tempted to resort to seeking photocopies of documents which can be examined at greater leisure outside the repositories. However, the provision of photocopies, and the whole area of reprography generally, can pose problems for the uninitiated student. Most repositories will no longer photocopy manuscript material, on conservation grounds, but they may offer, as alternatives, the provision of a photograph, a microfilm or microfilm printout. However, the provision of any copy, without the permission of the owner of the copyright of the manuscript, constitutes a breach of copyright which is an offence in law. In the case of Church of Ireland records there are a number of copyright owners. The older parish registers (registers of baptisms and marriages up to the end of 1870 and marriages before 1845) are state copyright in the Republic of Ireland and crown copyright in Northern Ireland and the permission of the National Archives and the Public Record Office in Belfast, respectively, is required before copies from these records may be obtained. Similarly the copyright of civil registers of marriage (those from 1845 on) is controlled by the Registrars General in Dublin and Belfast. The copyright of virtually all the remaining archives of parishes, dioceses, cathedrals and central church bodies is vested in the Representative Church Body and is administered through the Librarian and Archivist in the Representative Church Body Library in Dublin. In the case of the papers of organizations and individuals which have been deposited in libraries and archives the copyright, unless specifically assigned to a repository, usually remains with those who created the records or their heirs in law, and it is the responsibility of the custodian of the records to ensure that there are no avoidable breaches of copyright. Most problems in the copyright area arise not with a refusal to copy a document for research purposes, for adequate notes can usually be made, but with requests for illustrative material for publication. In most cases the Representative Church Body seeks to be accommodating in the cases in which it owns the copyright of documents, portraits and photographs, but frequently the copyright is someone else's property and in such circumstances the responsibility devolves on those who are seeking a copy to provide written permission from the copyright owner. If permission is granted for a copy to be made for a researcher there will, almost invariably, be a cost which must be passed on to the student. This may simply be the cost of providing the copy, but, in the case of all but the large national institutions, it is frequently more substantial than the average student, used only to subsidised photocopying charges in colleges, may be prepared for. If material has already been photographed or microfilmed the costs of providing prints or printouts from negatives are not considerable but if the documents have to photographed or microfilmed for the first time then the cost of these operations will usually be passed on to the person who requested the copies. Since such operations will usually involve contracting the work out to professionals the costs may on occasions be considerable and students would be wise to obtain an estimate before ordering any illustrative material. Some repositories will allow readers to take their own photographs under supervision but this option cannot be relied on. Finally, researchers should realise that most copyright owners are now aware that archives and their copyright are assets and, in an age of growing pressure for repositories to generate income, there is an increasing tendency to require the payment of reproduction fees.

Conclusion

The Church of Ireland, as the legal lineal descendant of the early Irish Church, has inherited responsibility for a collection of archives and manuscripts which are an important part of the national heritage. Despite losses of significant parts of the collection through accident, neglect and the periodic instability to which Irish society was subject, there remains in the custody of the Church and in the libraries of other institutions, to which items have strayed throughout the ages, a body of manuscript material, the understanding of which is essential for any effective analysis of the history of Irish society. Because the Church was organized locally through parishes, dioceses and cathedrals its records are particularly valuable for those engaged in the study of local history and because the Church of Ireland became the official church of the state it had a presence throughout the country which was more widespread and more influential than its position, as a minority Church, would otherwise have made possible.

The surviving body of records, substantial though it is, is only a fraction of that which once existed but information which has been lost can, to some extent, be recovered through the use of copies and extracts and by exploring supplementary sources such as inscriptions on gravestones, memorials and plate, and the evidence of archaeology and architecture. In addition, the pioneering work of scholars, principally in the late nineteenth and early twentieth centuries, in producing printed editions and calendars of archives and manuscripts has saved for posterity texts which otherwise would have been lost, especially in the light of the archival holocaust in the Four Courts in Dublin in 1922.

Subsequent work by scholars, archivists, librarians and committed amateur historians has produced a, by now, substantial body of catalogues, guides, lists and descriptive articles which can be used to interpret, in part, a wide variety of Church of Ireland archives and manuscripts. However, much material has yet to be catalogued and, given the unpredictable nature of Irish archival life, perhaps some valuable material may remain to be discovered. In both these fields of endeavour local historians have a valuable role to play. They, through their interest and enthusiasm, can set an agenda for local research to which archivists and librarians can, within the constraints under which they work, respond. More importantly, perhaps, they can, through their experience and expertise, help to develop a greater awareness of the centrality of Church of Ireland records to much local research. Together, those who have custody of the archives and manuscripts of the Church of Ireland and those who use them can be a formidable force for the development of local studies in Ireland.

Notes

CHAPTER ONE

1 For explanations of ecclesiastical termi-
nology, with bibliographical references,
see F.L. Cross and E.A. Livingstone
(ed.), *The Oxford dictionary of the
Christian church* (3rd ed., Oxford, 1997).

2 For a short introduction to the parish
system see G.W.O. Addleshaw, *The
beginnings of the parochial system* (London,
1953) and *The development of the parochial
system from Charlemagne (768–814) to
Urban II (1088–1099)* (London, (1954).

3 For an overview of Irish medieval
manuscripts see the series of Thomas
Davis lectures *Great books of Ireland*
(Dublin, 1967); Françoise Henry and
Genevive Marsh-Micheli, 'Manuscripts
and Illuminations, 1169–1603' in Art
Cosgrove (ed.), *A new history of
Ireland, II. Medieval Ireland, 1169–1534*
(Oxford, 1987), pp 780–815.

4 For a full discussion of the development of cathedral life see Kathleen
Edwards, *The English secular cathedrals in
the middle ages* (2nd ed., Manchester,
1967); S.E. Lemberg, *The reformation of
cathedrals. Cathedrals in English society,
1485–1603* (Princeton, 1988).

5 A.J. Otway-Ruthven, *A history of
medieval Ireland* (London, 1968), ch. iv.

6 Representative Church Body Library
(hereinafter R.C.B. Library) P326.

7 Trinity College, Dublin (hereinafter
T.C.D.) MS 1477. See also J.L.
Robinson, 'On the ancient deeds of
the parish of St John, Dublin' in
Proceedings of the Royal Irish Academy
(hereinafter *R.I.A. Proc.*) xxxiii, sect. C,
no. 7 (1916), pp 175–224.

8 See William Hawkes, 'The Liturgy in
Dublin, 1200–1500: manuscript
sources' in *Reportorium Novum*, ii, no. 1,
(1957–8), pp 33–67.

9 R.C.B. Library P117/12/1.

10 See H.F. Twiss, 'Some ancient deeds of
the parishes of St Catherine and St
James, Dublin'in *R.I.A. Proc.*, xxv, sect.
C, no. 7 (1919), pp 265–81 and 'Some
ancient deeds of the parish of St
Werburgh, Dublin' in *R.I.A. Proc.*, xxv,
sect. C, no. 8 (1919), pp 282–315.

11 Public Record Office of Northern
Ireland (hereinafter P.R.O.N.I.)
DIO4/2/1–13. See also note 139.

12 R.C.B. Library D6/1. See also note 140.

13 R.C.B. Library D6/3. See also note
140.

14 R.C.B. Library D11/1/2. See also note
141.

15 Limerick Diocesan Archives. See also
note 142.

16 R.C.B. Library C2/1/1. See also note
146.

17 Cambridge University Library Add
MS 710. See also note 147.

18 R.C.B. Library C6/1/1–2. See also note
143.

19 See note 141.

20 See Hawkes, op. cit.

21 T.C.D. MS 576.

22 R.C.B. Library C6/1/6/1–3.

23 See the appendices to the 20th, 23rd,
24th & 27th *Report of the deputy keeper
of the public records . . . Ireland*, (Dublin,
1888, 1891–2, 1895). A new and
expanded edition is M.J. McEnery and
Raymond Refaussé (ed.), *Christ
Church deeds* (Dublin, 2000).

24 *Calendar of entries in the papal registers
relating to Great Britain and Ireland*,
(ed.) W.H. Bliss (Vols I and II), W.H.
Bliss and C. Johnston (Vol. III), W.H.
Bliss and J.A. Twemlow (Vols IV and
V), J.A. Twemlow (Vols VI–XIV), M.J.
Haren (Vols XV and XVIII and XIX),
Anne P. Fuller (Vol. XVI) (London and
Dublin, 1893–1998).

25 M.P. Sheehy (ed.), *Pontifica Hibernica*
    (2 vols, Dublin, 1962 and 1965).

26 See above, p. 2 and below p. 36.

27 Peter Harbison, *The high crosses of
    Ireland* (3 vols, Bonn, 1992).

28 Roger Stalley, *The Cistercian monasteries of
    Ireland* (London and New Haven, 1987).

29 Elizabeth Fitzpatrick and Caimin
    O'Brien, *The medieval churches of
    County Offaly* (Dublin, 1998).

30 For a fuller introduction to the
    administration of the established
    church see D.H. Akenson, *The Church
    of Ireland. Ecclesiastical reform and
    revolution, 1800–1885* (New Haven and
    London, 1971), which despite its title,
    provides a useful overview of the
    eighteenth century.

31 The most recent listing of parish
    registers is Noel Reid (ed.), *A table of
    Church of Ireland parochial registers and
    copies* (Naas, 1994). See note 154 for a
    list of the publications of the Parish
    Register Society of Dublin.

32 For an introduction to the artistic
    significance of gravestones and
    memorials see Homan Potterton, *Irish
    church monuments, 1570–1880* (Belfast,
    1985) and Raymond Gillespie, 'Irish
    Funeral Monuments and Social
    Change, 1500–1700' in B.P. Kennedy
    and Raymond Gillespie (ed.), *Ireland.
    Art into history* (Dublin, 1994).

33 See text, pp 39–40.

34 The workings of the Irish vestries have
    yet to be adequately researched. An
    introduction to them may be had from
    Akenson, *The Church of Ireland* and
    Virginia Crossman, *Local government in
    nineteenth-century Ireland* (Belfast, 1994).

35 Peter Hart, *The IRA and its enemies:
    violence and community in Cork,
    1916–1923* (Oxford, 1998).

36 See text, pp 43–4.

37 The State Papers, Ireland and Home
    Office Papers, Ireland (National Library
    of Ireland microfilm collection).

38 R.C.B. Library D12.

39 For a fuller discussion of testamentary
    records, see Rosemary ffolliott and
    Eileen O'Byrne, 'Wills and
    Administrations' in D.F. Begley (ed.),
    Irish genealogy. A record finder (Dublin,
    1981), pp 157–180.

40 See text, pp 34–5.

41 See note 99.

42 Records of banns, either in the form
    of separate registers or as part of a
    parish register of baptisms, marriages
    and burials, are usually found among
    parish record collections. However,
    they rarely pre-date the nineteenth
    century.

43 See text, p. 41.

44 See note 113.

45 R.J. Hayes (ed.) *Manuscripts sources for
    the history of Irish civilization* (12 vols,
    Boston, 1964) and *Manuscript sources for
    the history of Irish civilization. First
    supplement, 1965–1975* (3 vols, Boston,
    1979) is still the best guide to such
    material.

46 R.C.B. Library MS 566.

47 The muniments of St Fin Barre's
    cathedral, Cork are in the cathedral.

48 R.C.B. Library C12.

49 R.C.B. Library C14.

50 See text, p.15.

51 Samuel Lewis, *A topographical dictionary
    of Ireland* (2 vols and atlas, London,
    1837).

52 See note 59.

53 R.C.B. Library P325/27/3.

54 R.C.B. Library C14.

55 St Fin Barre's Cathedral, Cork.

56 R.C.B. Library D6.

57 R.C.B. Library D5.

58 See text, p. 46.

59 R.C.B. Library D6.

60 P.R.O.N.I. DIO4/22.

61 R.C.B. Library C6/3.

62 R.C.B. Library C2.

63 *First report of His Majesty's
    Commissioners on Ecclesiastical Revenue
    and Patronage, Ireland* (1834); *Second
    report . . .* (1835); *Third report . . .* (1836);
    Fourth report . . . (1838).

64 The best guide to the administration
    of the disestablished Church is J.L.B.
    Deane, *Church of Ireland handbook* (2nd
    ed., Dublin, 1982).

65 A list of cases which were tried by the
    Court of the General Synod from 1885
    onwards is printed annually in the
    Journal of the General Synod.

66 Civil registration of protestant
    marriages began in 1845 and of all
    births, marriages and deaths in 1864.

These records have been collated and indexed in the General Register Office, Dublin.

67 Herbert Wood, *A guide to the records deposited in the Public Record Office of Ireland* (Dublin, 1919) is largely a catalogue of the records which were destroyed in 1922.

68 See text, pp 47–8.

69 See Raymond Refaussé, 'Church of Ireland Clerical Succession Lists and their Compilers' in *The Irish Genealogist*, x, no. 1 (1998), pp 32–41.

70 St J.D. Seymour, *The succession of parochial clergy in the united diocese of Cashel and Emly* (Dublin, 1908).

71 W.M. Brady, *Clerical and parochial records of Cork, Cloyne, and Ross* (Dublin, 1863–4).

72 H.B. Swanzy, *Succession lists of the diocese of Dromore* (Belfast, 1933).

73 W.H. Rennison, *Succession list of the bishops, cathedral and parochial clergy of the dioceses of Waterford and Lismore* (Ardmore, 1920).

74 J.B. Leslie, *Armagh clergy and parishes* (Dundalk, 1911); idem, *Clogher clergy and parishes* (Enniskillen, 1929); idem, *Ossory clergy and parishes* (Enniskillen, 1933); idem, *Ferns clergy and parishes* (Dublin, 1936); idem, *Derry clergy and parishes* (Enniskillen, 1937); idem, *Raphoe clergy and parishes* (Enniskillen, 1940); idem, Supplement to '*Armagh Clergy & Parishes*' (Dundalk, 1948); J.B. Leslie and H.B. Swanzy, *Biographical succession lists of the clergy of the diocese of Down* (Enniskillen, 1936).

75 R.C.B. Library MS 61.

76 See S.P. Lea, *The present state of the established church or ecclesiastical register of Ireland for the year 1814* (Dublin, 1814); J.C. Erck, *The Irish ecclesiastical register* (Dublin, 1817, 1818, 1820, 1825, 1830); J.M. Bourns, *The Irish clergy list and ecclesiastical almanack* (Dublin, 1843); *The Irish churchman's almanac* (Belfast, 1855); S.B. Oldham, *The clerical directory for Ireland* (Dublin, 1858).

77 See note 163.

CHAPTER TWO

1 Kenneth Milne, *The Church of Ireland. A history* (3rd ed., Dublin, 1994).

2 R.B. MacCarthy, *Ancient & modern. A short history of the Church of Ireland* (Dublin, 1995).

3 W.A. Phillips (ed.), *History of the Church of Ireland from the earliest times to the present day* (3 vols, Oxford, 1933).

4 D.H. Akenson, *The Church of Ireland*.

5 Deane, *Church of Ireland handbook*; W.G. Wilson, *How the Church of Ireland is governed* (Dublin, 1963).

6 *The Irish Builder* began life as *The Dublin Builder* in 1859 and changed its title in 1867.

7 A useful introduction to published works about the Church of Ireland is Alan Ford and Kenneth Milne (ed.), 'The Church of Ireland. A critical bibliography, 1536–1992' in *Irish Historical Studies*, xxviii, no. 112 (Nov. 1993), pp 345–84. For a comprehensive catalogue of shorter published works on Church of Ireland topics see R.J. Hayes (ed.), *Sources for the history of Irish civilization. Articles in Irish periodicals* (9 vols, Boston, 1970).

8 See note 45.

9 The National Register of Archives website address is www.hmc.gov.uk/nra/abtnra.htm

10 J.T. Gilbert, 'Archives of the see of Dublin' and 'Archives of the see of Ossory' in *Historical Manuscripts Commission, tenth report, appendix, pt. v* (London, 1885), pp 204–64.

11 J.T. Gilbert, 'Correspondence and papers of William King, archbishop of Dublin' in *Historical Manuscripts Commission, second report, appendix* (London, 1874), pp 231–62.

12 Seamus Helferty and Raymond Refaussé (ed.), *Directory of Irish Archives* (3rd ed., Dublin, 1999).

13 Mary Clark and Raymond Refaussé, *Directory of historic Dublin guilds* (Dublin, 1993).

14 For information on the records of guilds and confraternities outside Dublin see Hayes, *Manuscript sources for the history of Irish civilization*, v.

15 See in particular Colm Lennon, 'The chantries in the Irish Reformation: the case of St Anne's Guild, Dublin, 1550–1630' in R.V. Comerford et al (ed.), *Religion, conflict and coexistence in*

Ireland (Dublin, 1990); idem, 'The
survival of the confraternities in post-
Reformation Dublin' in *Confraternitas*,
vi, no. 1 (spring, 1995), pp 5–12.

16 T.K. Abbott, *Catalogue of the manuscripts
in the Library of Trinity College, Dublin*
Dublin, 1900).

17 M.L. Colker, *Trinity College Library
Dublin. Descriptive catalogue of the
medieval and renaissance Latin manuscripts*
(2 vols, Aldershot, 1991).

18 Douglas Hyde and D.J. O'Donoghue,
(comps), *Catalogue of the books and
manuscripts comprising the library of the
late Sir John T. Gilbert* (Dublin, 1918).

19 Rena Lohan, *Guide to the archives of the
Office of Public Works* (Dublin, 1994).

20 The Public Record Office of Ireland
and the State Paper Office were
amalgamated in 1986 to form the
National Archives.

21 Margaret Griffith, 'A short guide to the
Public Record Office of Ireland' in
Irish Historical Studies, viii, no. 29 (Mar.
1952), pp 45–58. A revised version of
this article was published in pamphlet
form in 1964.

22 *The Public Record Office. Sources for local
studies in the Public Record Office of
Ireland* (Dublin, 1982).

23 *An Irish genealogical source. Guide to
church records* (Belfast, 1993).

24 J.B. Leslie, *Catalogue of manuscripts in
possession of the Representative Church
Body . . . collected by the Ecclesiastical
Records Committee* (Dublin, 1938).

25 Geraldine Fitzgerald, 'Manuscripts in
the Representative Church Body
Library' in *Analecta Hibernica*, no. 23
(1966), pp 307–9.

26 Raymond Refaussé, 'The Swanzy
pedigree notebooks in the
Representative Church Body Library'
in *The Irish Genealogist* vi, no. 4 (1983)
pp 526–9; idem, 'The Welply will
abstracts' in *The Irish Genealogist* vi, no.
6 (1985), pp 814–23 and vii, no. 1
(1986), pp 113–21; idem, 'W.H. Welply's
pedigree notebooks' in *The Irish
Genealogist* vii, no. 3 (1987), pp 421–32;
idem, 'Marriage licences from the
Diocese of Ossory, 1739–1804' in *The
Irish Genealogist* viii, nos 1–3 (1990–92),
pp 122–44, 239–67, 393–428.

27 Susan Hood, 'The Diocesan Records
of Cloyne, County Cork' in *The Irish
Genealogist* ix, no. 4 (1997), pp 426–37.

28 Raymond Gillespie, 'The Archives of
Christ Church Cathedral, Dublin' in
Irish Archives, v, no. 2 (1998), pp 3–11.

29 Raymond Refaussé, 'The archives of
the Church of Ireland: an introduction' in *Irish Archives Bulletin* xi,
(1981), pp 3–11; idem, 'Sources for
labour history in the Representative
Church Body Library, Dublin' in
Saothar, no. 20 (1995), pp 95–6; idem,
'The Archives of the Church of Ireland
and the Representative Church Body
Library' in *Archivium Hibernicum*, xlix
(1995), pp 115–24.

30 For an overview of the diocesan
libraries see Maura Tallon, *Church of
Ireland diocesan libraries* (Dublin, 1959)
and Mary Casteleyn, *A history of
libraries in Ireland* (Aldershot, 1984),
pp 71–83.

31 N.J.D. White (ed.), *Catalogue of the
manuscripts remaining in Marsh's Library,
Dublin* (Dublin, n.d.). A revised edition
of this catalogue is also available on the
internet: the address of Marsh's Library
website is www.kst.dit.ie/marsh

32 James Dean, *Catalogue of manuscripts in
the Public Library of Armagh*
(Dundalk, 1928).

33 J.R. Garstin, 'Descriptive catalogue of
the Bishop Reeves' collection of
manuscripts' in *Down and Connor and
Dromore Diocesan Library. Catalogue of
books in the diocesan collections . . .*
(Belfast, 1899). This material has since
been deposited in P.R.O.N.I..

34 R.G.S. King, *St Columb's Cathedral,
Londonderry. Chapter House Library.
Short title catalogue* (Londonderry,
1939).

35 *Catalogue of the Cashel Diocesan Library*
(Boston, 1973).

36 H.W. Love, *Records of the archbishops of
Armagh being an indexed catalogue
of the manuscripts, documents and books in
the archiepiscopal registry of Armagh*
(Dundalk, 1965).

37 Published as appendices to the 26th
and 30th *Report of the deputy keeper of
the Public Records . . . Ireland* (Dublin,
1895 and 1899).

38 Arthur Vicars, *Index to the prerogative wills of Ireland, 1536–1810* (Dublin, 1897).

39 H.F. Berry, *Register of wills and inventories of the diocese of Dublin . . . 1457–1483* (Dublin, 1898).

40 H.B. Gillman, *Index to the marriage licence bonds of the diocese of Cork and Ross . . . 1623–1750* (Cork, 1896–7) and G.H. Green, *Index to the marriage licence bonds of the diocese of Cloyne . . . 1630–1800* (Cork, 1899–1900).

41 W.P.W. Phillimore (ed.), *Indexes to Irish wills. i. Ossory, Leighlin, Ferns, Kildare* (London, 1909); *ii. Cork and Ross, Cloyne* (London, 1910); Gertrude Thrift (ed.), *Indexes to Irish wills. iii. Cashel and Emly, Waterford and Lismore, Killaloe and Kilfenora, Limerick, Ardfert and Aghadoe* (London, 1913); *iv. Dromore, Newry and Mourne* (London, 1918); *v. Derry and Raphoe* (London, 1920).

42 Wallace Clare, *A guide to copies and abstracts of Irish wills* (reprint, Baltimore, 1989).

43 These are listed in D.F. Begley (ed.), *Irish genealogy*, pp 167–70.

44 Raymond Refaussé, 'Records of the Church of Ireland' in J.G. Ryan (ed.), *Irish church records* (Dublin, 1992), pp 41–68.

45 R.W. Dudley Edwards and Mary O'Dowd, *Sources for early modern Irish history, 1534–1641* (Cambridge, 1985).

46 Raymond Refaussé, 'Church Records' in William Nolan and Anngret Simms (ed.), *Irish towns: a guide to sources* (Dublin, 1988), pp 137–46.

47 William Nolan, *Tracing the past: sources for local studies in the Republic of Ireland* (Dublin, 1982).

48 T.P. O'Neill, *Sources of Irish local history* (Dublin, 1958).

49 J.G. Ryan, *Irish records. Sources for family and local history* (Dublin, 1988).

50 John Grenham, *Tracing your Irish ancestors* (Dublin, 1992).

51 Brian Mitchell, *A new genealogical atlas of Ireland* (Baltimore, 1988).

52 B.C. O'Donovan and David Edwards, *British sources for Irish history, 1485–1641. A guide to manuscripts in local, regional and specialised repositories in England, Scotland and Wales* (Dublin, 1997).

53 *Papers of British churchmen, 1780–1940* (London, 1987).

54 There are a number of editions of the Book of Kells of which the 1990 facsimile edition, with an accompanying volume of commentary edited by Peter Fox, is the most complete.

55 A.A. Luce, G.O. Simms, P. Meyer, L. Bieler, *Evangeliorum quattuor codex Durmacensis* (2 vols, Olten, Lausanne and Freiburg, 1960).

56 John Gwynn (ed.), *The book of Armagh* (Dublin, 1913).

57 F.E. Warren (ed.), *The antiphonary of Bangor* (2 vols, London, 1893 and 1895).

58 R.I. Best and H.J. Lawlor (ed.), *The martyrology of Tallaght* (London, 1831).

59 H.J. Lawlor, 'The Kilcormac Missal' in *Transactions of the Royal Irish Academy*, xxxi, pt x (Dublin, 1900), pp 393–430.

60 Charles Plummer, *Bethada Naem nErenn. Lives of the Irish saints* (2 vols, Oxford, 1922).

61 Gearóid MacNiocaill, *The medieval Irish annals* (Dublin, 1975).

62 Brendan Smith (ed.), *The register of Milo Seeetman . . . 1361–1380* (Dublin, 1996); H.J. Lawlor 'A Calendar of the register of Archbishop Fleming' in *R.I.A. Proc.*, xxx, sect. C, no. 5 (Dublin, 1912); D.A. Chart (ed.), *The register of John Swayne . . . 1418–1439* (Belfast, 1935); W.G.H. Quigley and E.F.D. Roberts (ed.), *Registrum Johannis Mey . . . 1443–1439* (Belfast, 1972); L.P. Murray, 'Archbishop Cromer's Register' in *Louth Arch. Soc. Jn.*, vi and vii (1926–30).

63 J.T. Gilbert, *Crede Mihi* (Dublin, 1897); Charles McNeill (ed.), *Calendar of Archbishop Alen's register* (Dublin, 1950).

64 H.J. Lawlor, 'Calendar of the Liber Ruber of the diocese of Ossory' in *R.I.A. Proc.*, xxvii, sect. C, no. 5 (1908), pp 159–208.

65 James McCaffrey (ed.), *The black book of Limerick* (Dublin, 1907).

66 H.J. Lawlor, 'A Calendar of the Liber Niger and Liber Albus of Christ Church, Dublin' in *R.I.A. Proc.*, xxvii, sect. C, no. 1 (1908), pp 1–93. Lawlor's calendar should be used in association with Aubrey Gwynn (ed.), 'Some unpublished texts from the Black

Book of Christ Church, Dublin' in
Annalecta Hibernica, no. 16 (1946),
pp 281–337.

67 J.C. Crosthwaite (ed.), *The book of obits
and martyrology of the cathedral of the
Holy Trinity, Dublin* (Dublin, 1844). A
more recent edition of the book of
obits is contained in Raymond
Refaussé and Colm Lennon (ed.), *The
registers of Christ Church Cathedral,
Dublin* (Dublin, 1998).

68 James Mills (ed.), *Account roll of the
priory of the Holy Trinity, Dublin,
1337–1346* (Dublin, 1891). A new
edition of Mill's work was published in
1996 with introductions by James
Lydon and A.J. Fletcher.

69 N.B. White (ed.), *The 'Dignitas Decani'
of St Patrick's Cathedral, Dublin*
(Dublin, 1957).

70 *Le tropaire-prosaire de Dublin* (Rouen,
1966).

71 J.T. Gilbert (ed.), *Chartularies of St
Mary's Abbey, Dublin* (2 vols, Dublin,
1884).

72 Richard Butler (ed.), *Registrum prioratus
omnium sanctorum* (Dublin, 1845).

73 J.T. Gilbert (ed.), *Register of the abbey of
St Thomas, Dublin* (Dublin, 1889).

74 M.V. Clarke, *Register of the priory of the
Blessed Virgin Mary at Tristernagh*
(Dublin, 1941).

75 E.St J. Brooks (ed.), *The Irish cartularies
of Llanthony prima & secundus*
(Dublin, 1953).

76 K.W. Nicholls, 'The Episcopal rentals
of Clonfert and Kilmacduagh' in
Analecta Hibernica, no. 26 (1970),
pp 103–143.

77 J. Mills (ed.), *The registers of St John the
Evangelist, Dublin, 1619–1699* (Dublin,
1906), *The register of the liberties of
Cashel, 1654–1657* (Dublin, 1907), *The
registers of St Peter and St Kevin, Dublin,
1663–1761* (Dublin, 1911); J.H. Bernard
(ed.), *The Registers of St Patrick, Dublin,
1677–1800* (Dublin, 1907); H.J. Lawlor
(ed.), *The registers of Provost Winter
(Trinity College, Dublin), 1650–1660*
(Dublin, 1907); H.S. Guinness (ed.),
*The register of the union of Monkstown
(Co. Dublin), 1669–1786* (Dublin, 1908);
H. Wood (ed.), *The registers of St
Catherine, Dublin, 1636–1715* (Dublin,

1908); H.F. Berry (ed.), *The registers of
St Michan, 1636–1700* (Dublin, 1909);
R. Hayes (ed.), *The register of Derry
cathedral . . . , 1642–1703* (Dublin, 1910);
D.A. Chart (ed.), *Marriage entries from
the registers of St Andrew, St Anne, St
Audoen & St Bride, 1632–1800* (Dublin,
1913); A.E. Langman (ed.), *Marriage
entries in the registers . . . S. Marie, S.
Luke, S. Catherine & S. Werburgh,
1627–1800* (Dublin, 1915).

78 Raymond Refaussé (ed.), *Register of the
parish of St Thomas, Dublin, 1750–1791*
(Dublin, 1994) and *Register of the church
of St Thomas, Lisnagarvey, Co. Antrim,
1637–1646* (Dublin, 1996); Colin
Thomas (ed.), *Register of the cathedral
church of St Columb, Derry, 1703–1732*
(Dublin, 1997) and *Register of the
cathedral church of St Columb, Derry,
1732–1775* (Dublin, 1999); Susan Hood
(ed.), *Register of the parish of Holy
Trinity, Cork, 1643–1668* (Dublin, 1998).

79 Herbert Wood (ed.), *Court book of the
liberty of Saint Sepulchre . . . 1586–1590*
(Dublin, 1930).

80 T.A. Lunham (ed.), 'Bishop Dive
Downes's visitation of his diocese,
1699' in *Cork Hist. Soc. Jn.* vols xiv and
xv (1908–9).

81 Raymond Gillespie (ed.), *The proctor's
accounts of Peter Lewis, 1574–1575*
(Dublin, 1996): idem (ed.), *The first
chapter act book of Christ Church
cathedral, Dublin, 1574–1634* (Dublin,
1997); idem, *Thomas Howell and his
friends: serving Christ Church cathedral,
Dublin, 1570–1700* (Dublin 1997);
'Borrowing books from Christ
Church' in *Long Room*, no. 43 (1998).

82 Raymond Refaussé, 'The Visitation
Note Book of Charles Lindsay, Bishop
of Kildare, 1804–1808' in *Kildare Arch.
Soc. Jn.*, xvii (1991).

83 M.V. Ronan, 'Archbishop Bukley's
Visitation of Dublin, 1630' in
Archivium Hibernicum, viii (1941).

84 R.J. Hayes (ed.), *Sources for the history
of Irish civilization. Articles in Irish
periodicals.*

85 R.S.J. Clarke (ed.), *Gravestone
inscriptions, County Down*, (20 vols,
Belfast, 1986–89); idem, *Gravestione
inscriptions, County Antrim* (3 vols

Belfast, 1977–95); idem, *Gravestone inscriptions, Belfast* (4 vols, Belfast, 1982–91).

86 The work of Cantwell and Egan is available in typescript in the major Dublin repositories.

87 C.A. Webster, *The church plate of the diocese of Cork, Cloyne and Ross* (Cork, 1909).

88 St J.D. Seymour, *Church plate and parish records, diocese of Cashel and Emly* (Clonmel, 1930).

89 Tony Sweeny, *Irish Stuart silver. Catalogue raisonné* (Dublin, 1995).

90 *Lists of oil paintings, mezzoinits . . . in possession of the bishops, deans, chapters and Representative Body of the Church of Ireland* (Dublin, 1916).

91 *Church disestablishment 1870–1970. A centenary exhibition* (Dublin, 1970).

92 National Archives Acc. No. 1045.

93 National Library of Ireland (hereinafter N.L.I.) PC 227.

94 Toby Barnard, 'Learning, the learned and literacy in Ireland, *c.* 1660–1760' in Toby Barnard, Dáibhí Ó Cróinín and Katherine Simms (ed.), *A miracle of learning . . . Essays in honour of William O'Sullivan* (Aldershot, 1998), pp 209–35.

95 N.L.I. MS: unlisted collection.

96 See D.A. Cronin, *A Galway gentleman in the age of improvement. Robert French of Monivea, 1716–79* (Dublin, 1995).

97 http://proni.nics.gov.uk/index.htm

98 P.R.O.N.I. D664, D3279

99 P.R.O.N.I. D10/1

100 P.R.O.N.I. M1C/520

101 P.R.O.N.I. D10/1

102 P.R.O.N.I. D/4179 respectively.

103 Details of clerical fellows who resigned to take up parochial appointments may be had from J.R. Bartlett (ed.), *Trinity College, Dublin Record Volume 1991* (Dublin, 1992).

104 T.C.D. MSS 2321a, 6396–7.

105 T.C.D. MS 4326.

106 T.C.D. MSS 4024, 4026–31, 4033, 4037, 5118.

107 T.C.D. MSS 2288 and 2288a.

108 T.C.D. MSS 2904–11, 3760.

109 T.C.D. MSS 2010–15.

110 T.C.D. MSS 7644–62.

111 T.C.D. MSS 7664–8.

112 T.C.D. MSS 5134–5202d.

113 Royal Irish Academy (hereinafter R.I.A.) MS 4. B. 36.

114 R.I.A. MS 24.Q.32–3.

115 R.I.A. MS 12.D.25.

116 R.I.A. MS 24.K.25.

117 Angélique Day and Patrick McWilliams (ed.), *Ordnance survey memoirs of Ireland* (40 vols, Belfast 1990–98).

118 http://www.ireland.anglican.org/

119 Registers of baptisms and burials up to and including the year 1870 and registers of marriages before the introduction of civil registration of protestant marriages in 1845.

120 R.C.B. Library MS 138.

121 R.C.B. Library MS 139.

122 R.C.B. Library: records of the Representative Church Body.

123 R.C.B. Library MS 328.

124 R.C.B. Library MS 183.

125 R.C.B. Library MS 440.

126 R.C.B. Library MS 117.

127 R.C.B. Library MS 262.

128 R.C.B. Library MS 11 and 581.

129 R.C.B. Library MS 40.

130 R.C.B. Library MS 550.

131 R.C.B. Library MS 486.

132 The record of the Protestant Orphan Society for counties Carlow (MS 340), Cork (MS 519), Kerry (MS 527), Meath (MS 286), Offaly (Ms 501) and Sligo (MS 416) have been deposited in the R.C.B. Library.

133 R.C.B. Library MS 485.

134 R.C.B. Library MS 263.

135 R.C.B. Library MS 551.

136 T.C.D. MSS 5225–5859 and R.C.B. Library MS 151.

137 R.C.B. Library MS 154.

138 R.C.B. Library MS 357.

139 R.C.B. Library MS 523.

140 R.C.B. Library MS 354.

141 See note 108.

142 http://www.ireland.anglican.org/

CHAPTER THREE

1 J.H. Baxter and Charles Johnston, *Medieval Latin word-list from British and Irish sources* (London, 1934).

2 For example, E.E. Thoyts, *How to read old documents* (Christchurch, 1972) provides a commentary on various types of documents with illustrations of different types of writing and tables of letter shapes, as does L.C. Hector, *The handwriting of English documents* (Dorking, 1980).